A Look to the Past

Kirkland

by

Matthew W. McCauley

Foreword by Alan J. Stein

A Look to the Past: Kirkland

Copyright © 2011 by Matthew W. McCauley

ISBN-10: 1453884882
ISBN-13: 978-1453884881

Second Edition
Scriptoria Publications
Auburn, WA 98001
(253) 804-2631
Author contact: javafour@aol.com

Cover: Peter Kirk's Great Western Iron & Steel Company steel mill, about 1891. The mill was constructed to produce railroad rails, but never produced a single one. It was located on Rose Hill, near Forbes Lake and the Kirkland Costco store.

Contents

To the incredible Dr. Angel W.

Without her wonderful inspiration this project would
have remained on my To Do List into perpetuity.

Foreword

It is a pleasure having Matt McCauley's *A Look to the Past* articles finally gathered together in one volume. When they were first published in the *Kirkland Courier* two decades ago, they were such a joy to read that I saved most of them in my clippings file. I say "most" because I now see that I missed a few, and I was delighted to read some "new" ones after all these years. What a treat.

I met Matt back in the early 1990s, when I joined the Kirkland Heritage Society (KHS). At the time, I was helping to create an index of the old *East Side Journal* newspaper – a project begun by Dr. Lorraine McConaghy. I was new to Kirkland, and because the city's history was then a blank slate to me, I relished poring over the newspapers, entering every headline from 1918-1975 into a database. Three or four nights a week, I'd head down to the Kirkland Library, where a pre-internet computer and a microfilm reader were set aside for my use.

Each month, when I attended KHS meetings, I'd bring along some tidbits that I had found to share with the members. These printouts always seemed to elicit discussions and evoke memories from quite a few of the seniors in attendance, but the most interesting articles were of stories that had long since been forgotten or overlooked. Everyone was intrigued by those, especially Matt, who always wanted to find out more about these strange glimpses into Kirkland's past.

Matt and I became good friends almost immediately. His fascination with Eastside history was nearly life-long, and he was as intrigued with digging up new information as I was. As work progressed on the *East Side Journal* database, I'd frequently head over to his house with a stack of article printouts, which we'd analyze and discuss for hours. Matt had a knack for cross-referencing some of these stories with historic photographs from the KHS collection, along with his own research into Kirkland and Eastside history.

Around this time, Matt launched and began editing *Blackberry Preserves*, the KHS newsletter. In it, he would often feature a photo, and then provide background info based on newspaper articles, oral histories, and other resources. I looked forward to each publication to see what stories he'd tell next. A lot of other people did too, and the newsletter proved to be such a success, that he began writing articles for the *Kirkland Courier*. You now hold those in your hands.

As you read through these essays, take note of the little details that Matt sometimes points out in the photos – details you might otherwise miss without his guiding hand. And be sure to look closely at the other historic photos he's added to accent some of the articles. But most of all enjoy the tales he weaves throughout. The secret to good history is good storytelling, and using each main image as a springboard, Matt launches into just that.

Alan Stein

November 8, 2010

Alan J. Stein is a HistoryLink.org staff historian, and is the award-winning author of *Safe Passage: The Birth of Washington State Ferries, 1951–2001*; *Bellevue Timeline: The Story of Washington's Leading Edge City from Homesteads to High Rises, 1863–2003*; and *The Olympic: The Story of Seattle's Landmark Hotel*. His most recent book, which he co-authored with Paula Becker, is *Alaska-Yukon-Pacific Exposition; Washington's First World's Fair*.

Preface

I should explain what this book is and what it is not.

This is *not* a comprehensive history of the City of Kirkland, though I believe that since 35 years and several annexations have elapsed since such a work was last published, Kirkland is certainly due for one.

This book is not a scholarly project. It is journalistic in approach and style, so I have omitted formal citations to authority. I have attributed many sources within the columns, but with most of the unattributed background, do know that I relied on primary sources.

A Look to the Past: Kirkland is a collection of 50 Kirkland history columns of that name that I wrote for the *Kirkland Courier* in 1993 and 1994. For the most part I have left them as published, with minor corrections, updates, and where appropriate, added information. I have also added images that were not present in the original columns (the tight limitations of newspaper space gave me only one image per column).

In 1993, I had completed my journalism studies at Seattle University, and was writing wire radio news for United Press International and preparing to attend Seattle University School of Law. Because of my lifelong fascination with Eastside history, in the early 1990s I participated in the resurrection of the old Kirkland Heritage Commission (KHC), re-established as the Kirkland Heritage Society. This effort was led by Barbara Loomis, with the help of Dale and Loita Hawkinson, Bob Burke, Sue Carter, and other 1970s-era KHC members.

As the Kirkland Heritage Society came into being I had the opportunity to explore the modest assortment historic photographs and materials that KHC has collected two decades earlier and I began to research the area's past. Excited by what I was learning and hoping to share it with others, in early 1993 I obtained the enthusiastic support of KHS directors and launched the organization's publication, *Blackberry Preserves* (BP). BP was a standard newsletter, reporting on KHS's operational issues, but I also used it as a platform to publish articles and images about Kirkland-area history.

BP was very well received and went on to win the Washington Trust for Historic Preservation Award for Excellence in Communications in October, 1994. Credit for what it became lies with all those who contributed content. One early contributor was noted local history writer Alan J. Stein, who has since gone on to publish several books on local history and is now a staff historian at HistoryLink.org and writer.

As BP developed momentum, the *Kirkland Courier*'s then-editor, Andrew Tarica, and I discussed offering my research as a weekly column and *A Look to the Past* was born. I had a great time researching and writing these columns and along the way met some incredible Kirkland seniors who were kind enough to share their time, memories, and family photographs with me. Through the process of meeting these wonderful folks I made some indescribable friendships and came to deeply appreciate where I was lucky enough to live.

By late 1994, the time demands on me--between law school and family obligations—became substantial and I had to discontinue my column, though KHS member Christina Brugman and others continued to write similar pieces in the *Courier* after I had to stop. I relocated to Baltimore, Maryland in 1996, for business reasons, returned to the Kirkland-area briefly between 2003 and 2005, and returned once again to Baltimore in 2005. In 2010, the context of my changed in such a way that I was able to permanently reestablish myself in Kirkland. This time I plan to stay a long, long time!

I long ago became a KHS life member and have kept abreast of its activities through BP even when I lived in the east. When I returned to Kirkland in 2010 I became active once more in KHS. A number of old friends urged me to re-publish my *A Look to the Past* columns, and this book is the result.

Kirkland is a great place to live, and it is so through the efforts of many people, past and present. These are the stories of some of those people. I hope you enjoy learning about their lives as much as I did.

I tip my cap to them all.

City's past explored in new column

Matt McCauley

A Look to the Past, the new history column in the "Kirkland Courier," began as a regular feature last week.

The idea behind the column came from longtime resident Matt McCauley, a member of the Kirkland Heritage Society and the editor of the group's newsletter.

McCauley — who studies journalism at the University of Washington — began to develop a love for history as a little boy, growing up in the Juanita area in the 1960s.

"I had a lot of neighbors who were elderly and were either settlers or descendants of settlers," said the 28-year-old McCauley.

His neighbors lived in farm houses, he said, and they used to spend hours telling story after story about old-time Kirkland.

"But they used to call all these places by different names from what I knew," McCauley said.

"For instance, they used the name Langdon Road rather than 116th Street. They used Vooris Road rather than 124th Street. And they used Juanita Junction rather than the intersection of 116th and Northeast 98th.

"So I guess that peaked my curiosity in history."

McCauley, who is a third generation Kirkland resident, has even taken his love for history to the depths of Lake Washington.

In 1984, he started a lake salvaging business, and dug out — among other odds and ends — five World War II airplanes, old bottles, and parts from long forgotten steamboat wrecks.

To create A Look to the Past, McCauley will take advantage of his access to hundreds of vintage photos on file at the Kirkland Heritage Society. He will also use his photography skills to document how these historical places look today.

"I think we can learn a lot about the past," he said, "and I think it should be appreciated.

"But in a way, it's also kind of like a treasure map where we can put all the pieces together, to come up with a conclusion about why certain areas are the way they are."

"A Look To The Past" was introduced in the August 11, 1993 issue of the *Kirkland Courier*, but had debuted the previous week. (The above story contains one minor error: the author attended Seattle University, not the University of Washington).

Preface to the Second Edition

I was delighted, profoundly flattered and, admittedly, somewhat surprised by the enthusiasm with which Kirklanders, past and present, received the first edition of *A Look to the Past: Kirkland*. Several groups asked me to make presentations about the book where interacting with readers and listening to their Kirkland memories was an amazing experience. At times it was quite moving.

An added bonus was that the book's Facebook fan page has attracted about 500 fans. In addition to current Kirkland residents it also permitted frequent communication with those who have left and scattered around the world, but who often still have images and strong memories to share of their time here. This connection with them fascinated and intrigued me—there is clearly no shortage of stories to tell about Kirkland's past!

With all this interaction with readers something became immediately obvious: The book should have been indexed.

Creating an index after-the-fact is an arduous process and given my time constraints this was a real challenge. Luckily, an amazing young woman undertook this substantial task.

Amy Seto Musser had earned a BFA in Theatre/Stage Management from Millikin University, in Decatur, Illinois. She was volunteering at the King County Library Kirkland Branch and working at the Kirkland Performance Center while pursuing her MLS (Masters in Library Science) with Texas Women's University. Amy expended countless hours going through the book, both compiling the index and noting other areas that needed attention. Her enthusiasm for the Kirkland community, for this project and her keen attention to detail proved an unbeatable combination and I must express my deepest appreciation for her invaluable contribution.

The other content addition is the story of the Clark Tragedy. Unlike the book's other vignettes, I wrote this piece in 2011 and published it on Kirklandviews.com, where I am a frequent poster and a contributing writer. Reaction to the article was substantial and emotional; most flattering is that Clark decedents expressed their approval and support. The Clark story brought unprecedented reader reaction and many conveyed to me that given the event's significance their story should be included with my early work. As a parent, it was the toughest Kirkland event I've ever researched and written about. It is my hope that this family can be honored in some small way by the City of Kirkland, perhaps naming after them a park, trail or other feature near their old homestead in the Highlands neighborhood, so that future generations of Kirklanders understand the drama that was the wilderness which became Kirkland.

The Clark article would likely not have been written but for my beautiful, inspiring and reflexively kind friend, Baltimore, Maryland, poet Marianne Reinsfelder. Thank you for that, MA.

Matt McCauley
November, 2011

Acknowledgments

I loved writing the newspaper columns that are the backbone of this book. I wrote them in the early 1990s, in what began as a journalistic writing project that rapidly became a labor of love and the gratification of my inborn curiosity about the place where I was raised. As I interviewed, one after another, so many of the people whose parents and grandparents settled this wonderful part of the world, I realized I was only one removed from actually witnessing Kirkland's history from its beginnings. It was a powerful feeling, and it is one of the things that draw people who love history, to history. Assembling these columns into this book, editing it, and adding photographs was still another trip back into time, but it was a lot more work and less fun, probably because I didn't get to interview people and learn new information, as I did when I wrote the columns. That said, it was a wonderful experience nonetheless, for it plunged me back, deeply, into the feeling of Kirkland. Every place has a feeling. When you are in your place and you feel it, it is a rich experience, and that is what I felt when I got into this project.

Numerous people helped make possible the writing of these columns and their collection into this volume, and I cannot list them all. But I will try. I thank my wonderful ex-wife and friend, Ashley Stark-McCauley. Back in early 1990s she was working on her Master's degree in English and teaching freshman comp at Western Washington University. Though she did not share my interest in or passion for Kirkland's history, her editorial assistance and objectivity and her critical eyes were invaluable. I also thank my father, William McCauley, for all his help, in the 1990s and with editorial assistance in compiling and publishing this collection.

I thank Amanda McQuay, a beautiful young woman in Baltimore, who—quite unintentionally— motivated me to return to Kirkland, the home I love. It is where I belong, and she helped push me in this direction. Both a mother and realtor extraordinaire, Amanda is exceptional, both professionally and personally. I adore her because she is provocative and original and curious all the while being both compassionate and reflexively kind.

For my early interest in Kirkland's past I thank Russ McClintick, Sr. and the late Donald Barrie. I attended Juanita's A.G. Bell Elementary from 1969-76 where Mr. Barrie was custodian. From 1970, Mr. McClintick was principal. Both men grew up in Kirkland, and their stories about Kirkland's past fired my imagination and my curiosity as a young boy attending Bell. They helped me to understand, at a young age, that Kirkland was a special place, and they motivated me to learn all I could about it.

The late Charles Fowler and his wife Helma lived next door to the house in which I lived in my first decade of life. They bought their house and property from a family that assembled the house from a Sears Roebuck kit in the 1910s. The Fowlers also sold four building sites to my grandfather in 1963. On those sites my father, my grandfather, my uncle, and my great uncle built houses. My grandparents and great uncle and great aunt are gone now, but my uncle still lives in one of the houses.

Charlie and Helma were married 1919, a year after Charlie returned from serving his country in Europe in World War I. My generation of McCauley kids (there were six of us on that hillside) knew them as "Grandma and Grandpa Fowler." They loved to share stories of their early lives in Kirkland.

When I was 10, I asked Grandpa Fowler if I could dig around in the earth behind his house, which was up the hill from ours about a hundred feet. I was convinced that I would discover treasures. Grandpa Fowler kindly allowed me to dig around behind their house. I unearthed treasures, alright—a rusty horse shoe, a rust-encrusted padlock, and several old paint cans (Grandpa Fowler was a house painter). These were indeed treasures in the eyes of a ten-year-old.

12

Barbara Loomis was the driving force behind the reorganized and reinvigorated Kirkland Heritage Society, resurrecting it from the moribund Kirkland Historic Commission in 1992. Another KHS past president, Bob Burke, also led the organization through incredible growth, and under his leadership an arrangement was made with the City of Kirkland, whereby Heritage Hall was moved to its current location at the foot of Market Street and the Heritage Resource Center was established. The city deserves kudos for making this possible. During Bob's tenure the KHS collections grew substantially and I have included many of those newly acquired images in this volume.

Alan Stein was indexing the old *East Side Journal* newspapers back in 1993-94 and his efforts helped many of these columns come to life. Alan has since gone on to publish four local history works. He has long held a staff position at HistoryLink.org, a wonderful online resource of Washington historical information. I also admire and respect the work of Dr. Lorraine McConaghy. In the early 1990s she led the Kirkland History Project through King County. I participated in that project as an oral history interviewer. I learned a lot from her and from that remarkable experience. Lorraine was instrumental in the creation of the *East Side Journal* database.

I also offer special thanks to my friends, current KHS president, Loita Hawkinson, and her husband Dale Hawkinson. They provided much support and encouragement for this project during the summer of 2010, and both made too many contributions to list. Loita is passionate and knowledgeable about Kirkland's history and Dale's sturdy efforts to make resources available through the internet were of immense value. I encourage everyone to view the material online at kirklandheritage.org. I am very happy to see that their outreach into the community has brought even more images and other items into the public realm.

David Sherbrooke's family goes back to its 1910s Sherbrooke Bulb Farm located behind the old Burke & Farrar Building at 1 Lake Street and adjacent to the Kirkland-Madison Park ferry dock that once stood at the foot of Kirkland Avenue. Dave, a retired Bellevue School District educator, provided some much appreciated copy editing.

I thank Rob Butcher, editor of KirklandViews.com, for regularly publishing my new articles about Kirkland's past. I also thank Carrie Wood, editor of the *Kirkland Reporter*—the successor newspaper to the old *Kirkland Courier*, where these articles first appeared—for also publishing my current feature columns.

Mary Harris and Rebecca Willow, co-owners of Kirkland's Parkplace Books, have been enormously supportive of promoting the story of Kirkland's past and of this project. Their store, now in its 25th year, is a Kirkland asset of immeasurable value and both women have decades of community service work--their efforts toward making Kirkland the wonderfully livable community we enjoy today are too numerous to list.

Matt McCauley,

May, 2011

Special Thanks

The following individuals and families provided images or other helpful information that informed this book. In many cases they loaned materials to the Kirkland Heritage Society for duplication or in some cases assisted me directly. When descendants decide to allow their family materials to be duplicated it is often a collective decision involving too many individuals to thank by name. In some cases, I have identified a member of the historic family who has provided notable assistance in getting their family's contribution to Kirkland's past documented through the KHS, or who gave me direct assistance. I should also clarify that some of the individuals named below are members of more than one historic Kirkland family. I urge anyone who has historic Kirkland materials to contact the Kirkland Heritage Society at (425) 827-3446 to arrange for duplication. The more information KHS has, the better it can accomplish its mission of documenting Kirkland's past. Please also remember that KHS is very interested in materials relating to newly annexed areas, including, but certainly not limited to, Finn Hill, Juanita, and Kingsgate.

Arlene André (also published as Arline Stokes and Arline Ely)

Barrie Family and Mabel and Donald Barrie

Forbes Family and Dorris Beecher

Ostberg, Johnson, and McAuliffe Families, and JoAnn McAuliffe, and special mention to Janice La Haye and Molly Bishop

Mickelson Family and Helen Mickelson

Charles Morgan

Higginbotham Family and Florence and Orval Higginbotham and Elaine Higginbotham

Lois Sundberg

Dorothy Daily

Sessions Family and Milt Sessions

Gary Lanksbury

City of Kirkland

Jerry Rutherford

Frank Rosin

Betty McClintick Gaudy

Ed King

Josten Family and Elaine McKenna

Marsh Family and Jerry Marsh

Carrilon Point

Edith Jewell Osborn

Stan Denton

Hansen Family and Carol Trapp

Pound Family and Thad Pound

McKibben Family and Dr. Ernest McKibben, Jr.

Gil Kvam

Don Sherwood

Donna Porter

Burr Family and Martha Burr Millar

Arden Olson

Robert Neir

Ernest Fortescue

Shinstrom Family and Pat and Dick Shinstrom

Robert Ely

Al Locke

Raine Family and Doris Snow

Wittenmyer Family and Glenn Eagon

Carr Family and Marie Peterson Yesland

Phillip Toman

Raymond Goings

Kirtley Family

Fish Family and Jean Olson

French and Davis Families

Arthur Knutson

Denton Family and Stan Denton

Clarence Stone

Glenn Landguth

Nancy Landguth Bock

Collins Family

Millie Ferguson Holmes

Everest Family and Ms Sarah Jane Everest

Tuttle and Stamp Families and Carylon Laskowski

Marilyn Timmerman Johnson

The Clark and Patty Families and Warren Fessenden, Patty Fessenden Bernhardt, Bruce Patty

Brooks Family and Margaret Gallegher Hassel and Laurie Klemmedson

Tillman Family and Mary Spiers Cazabon

Nancy Williams Bell

John Boykin

Capron Family and Victor Capron

Sue Carter

Merrily Hardenbrook Dicks

Janeen Wentz Ryseff

I must add a very special thanks to KHS President Loita Hawkinson not only for allowing me unfettered access to historical materials, but for reaching out to Kirkland's historic families, and facilitating the loan of family treasures to KHS. Loita makes certain that loaned items are well cared for while in KHS possession, she ensures they are properly duplicated and then, most importantly, promptly returns the materials to their owners.

KHS volunteer Christina Brugman has worked hard at acquiring photographs and oral histories, especially from the Kingsgate and Juanita neighborhoods, and the material she has recorded was of immeasurable value to me in updating many of these columns.

Finally, the images, extensive research, and related material collected by Arline André for her 1975 history of Kirkland, *Our Foundering Fathers,* which she published under the name Arline Ely, was of immense help to me in many areas of research over the past four decades—I have owned a copy since it was released in 1975. Much of her materials is now archived by KHS. Her daughters, Casey Stokes Miller and Kelly Stokes Hettinger, deserve and get my heartfelt thanks for assisting KHS in making sure her work remains accessible to the public.

Heritage Hall in 2010. Jake and Cam McCauley relax on the steps.

The Kirkland Heritage Society made this book possible. Without access to its extensive image and resource collection, *A Look to the Past: Kirkland* would not have happened.

KHS is based in its resource center in the lower level of Heritage Hall, located at 203 Market Street. For anyone interested in Kirkland's past I could not urge KHS membership more enthusiastically. Monthly dues are nominal and members receive a monthly award-winning newsletter, *Blackberry Preserves*, and monthly meetings offer programs of diverse subjects related to local history.

Kirkland is the most history-rich of Eastside communities—its heritage enhances dramatically the quality of life here and KHS works to document that heritage. Its mission is to identify Kirkland's many historic sites and to collect, preserve and interpret all elements of Kirkland's fascinating past. HKS seeks to promote public involvement in and appreciation of Kirkland's heritage.

KHS activities include providing exhibits at various public locations, including City Hall and Heritage Hall, conducting oral history interviews with area seniors, assisting in the research and preparation of interpretive historical markers and plaques, surveying and inventorying historic properties and sites within the city, assisting the City of Kirkland in planning and preservation, collecting images and other ephemera and making them available to the public, and providing scholarships.

KHS is based in Heritage Hall, a 1922 building that was for many years the First Church of Christ, Scientist, located about a block east its present location. It was moved in 1999. The KHS Resource Center serves as a work site and research area, it also contains a climate-controlled archive to house its various collections. For more information visit kirklandheritage.org or call (425) 827-3446.

KHS member Mr. Russell McClintick, Sr., at a 2010 KHS meeting, is seen identifying people in historic photos.

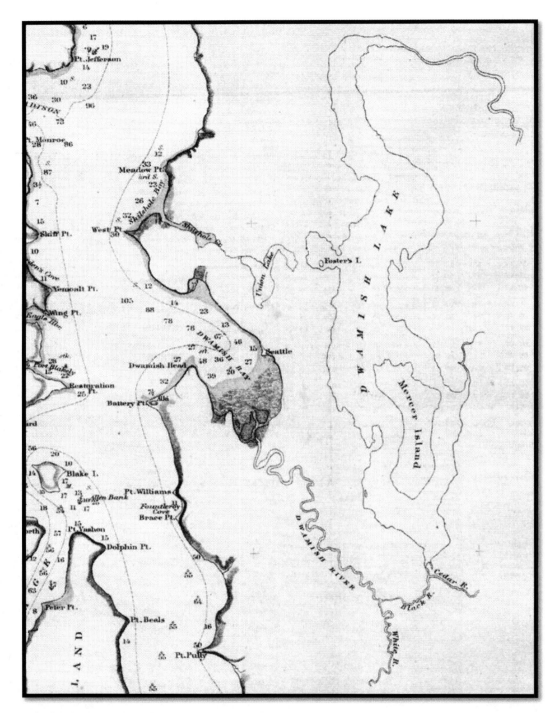

This 1867 nautical chart shows the area as the settlers found it. Lake Washington, then called Dwamish, was nine feet higher than it is today. The now-extinct Black River drained it into Elliott Bay. Seattle was a tiny village on the Duamish (then Dwamish) River mudflats. Other than beginning the development of the coalfields near Newcastle, settlers had little disturbed the thickly forested Eastside. By 1870 this would begin to change.

1890: Peter Kirk and the Great Western Iron & Steel Works

The Great Western Iron & Steel Company steel works, c. 1892. The planked road is today's Seventh Avenue, then called Picadilly. The mill was located on Rose Hill near today's intersection of 122nd Avenue NE and NE 90th Street, just northeast of where Costco's parking lot now stands.

Though the eighties was a decade of feverish speculation and development in Kirkland, an economic slump in the early nineties brought an end to the boom. Recent times? No. It was over 100 years ago, in the 1880s and 1890s. At the time, the centerpiece of Kirkland was to be the Great Western Iron & Steel Works—a mill that never produced a ton of steel.

In the mid-1880s, Kirkland comprised about 100 settlers who had built their homes in the dense, dark forest along the lakeshore from Houghton to Juanita Bay. Several of these settlers, such as Jay O'Conner and Dorr Forbes, were Civil War veterans. Most of the settlers lived off their land and picked up work where they could. The community had no grand design. In that context the planned development of the Great Western Iron & Steel Works was enormously important.

Lured by Seattle pioneer A.A. Denny's report of significant deposits of iron ore near Snoqualmie Pass, Peter Kirk, who came from Workington, England, toured the eastern lakeshore and other western Washington locations in 1886, looking for suitable location for the steel mill and town site that he envisioned. He made another trip to area in 1887, and by 1888 was in business.

With the encouragement of his new partner, *The Seattle Post-Intelligencer* publisher, Leigh S. J. Hunt (the Hunt's Point namesake), Kirk and his investors incorporated the Kirkland Land & Improvement Company in July, 1888. The company bought approximately 5,000 acres of property between Juanita Slough and Central Avenue, from the lake up Rose Hill, including today's Peter Kirk Park.

The land company investors created a second corporation in August, 1888, to establish the mill and engage in its operations as the Moss Bay Iron & Steel Company of America. The corporation's planners had originally wanted to put the mill in today's downtown Kirkland, but the Northern Pacific Railroad refused to run a rail spur any closer than Forbes Lake—so that is where they built the mill in 1891, on a 120 acre parcel provided by its sister corporation, the Kirkland Land & Improvement Company. The land company sought to develop its remaining acreage into a town site, named Kirkland, in Kirk's honor.

In 1889 financial trouble came to the steel mill enterprise, perhaps brought on by the disastrous Great Seattle Fire that year. All but one of the corporation's backers lived in Seattle and their finances were tied to the local economy. The corporation was unable to attract new capital, so a successor corporation was formed in June, 1890—the Great Western Iron & Steel Company. Much of its capital stock was held by prominent out-of-state financiers, investors brought aboard by Leigh Hunt. It is also worth noting that at that time Hunt, not Kirk, was the corporation's president. The stockholders pledged themselves to purchase $1 million of company stock. Thus capitalized, mill construction began and the future looked bright.

The town site was platted with its center at the intersection of Seventh and Market Streets, where the Peter Kirk, Joshua Sears, and Campbell buildings, built in 1890-91, stand today. Seventh Avenue—then called Picadilly—was a planked road leading up to the mill.

Other development and speculation flourished in Kirk's boomtown—now called Kirkland—and it seemed destined to become, as promised, the "Pittsburgh of the West." But, the Financial Panic of 1893 brought everything to a halt. Capital dried up before the investors could build the crucial rail line to the iron mines. No ore, no steel. No steel, no town.

Houses built west of Market Street — which had been selling for $950 in 1890— fell in value to $100 by 1894. Creditors auctioned off the mill machinery, and the building was boarded up and abandoned. Most of Kirkland's mill investors were ruined.

Through a twist of fate Kirk escaped bankruptcy. Before 1893 he had tried to liquidate his British assets to pump up his Kirkland ventures, but had been unsuccessful. This, it turned out, was his good fortune. Much of his wealth remained safe, back in England.

Kirk never gave up on Kirkland; he continued invest in the town right up to his death in 1916, shortly before the Lake Washington Ship Canal opened—a project Kirk believed would give Kirkland a second chance to become an important industrial center.

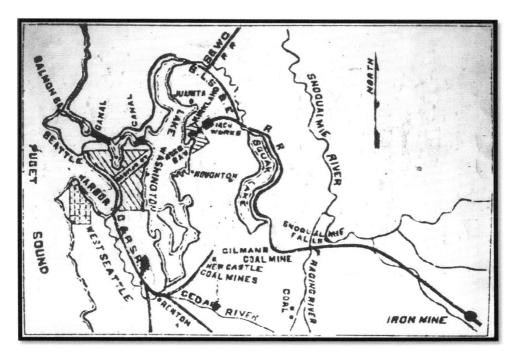

The developers' vision.

The Great Western Iron & Steel Company mill c. 1892, facing east. The front building contained the pattern shop on the left side, blacksmith shop in the center, and machine shop at the right.

Facing north, the stock bunker at far right was 350 feet long. The center building was the foundry and the building at the far left housed the machine, blacksmith, and pattern shops.

View looking east at the mill across Forbes Lake, then called Steel Works Lake and later known by Rose Hill neighbors as Little Lake, and also called Lake Kirkland for many years. This lake and Lake Washington had pump houses and pipelines to supply water to the mill. The structure center-left is the sawmill. The railbed is today's Slater Avenue.

23

Peter Kirk

Members of the Lee family in 1914 in the ruins of the stock bunker of the Great Western Iron & Steel Company steel mill. The machinery of the Great Western Iron & Steel Works was auctioned off years earlier in a sheriff's sale to satisfy corporate debts, much of which were owed to its sister corporation, the Kirkland Land & Improvement Company. The facility had included fully equipped foundry, machine, blacksmith, and pattern shops, as well as a saw mill used to supply the buildings' construction—it cut millions of board feet of timber from the immediate area. In addition to the specialized steel and iron processing equipment, such as blowing engine, roots blower, steam hammer, and Collian cupola furnace, there was a collection of drill presses, lathes, saws, boring mills, planers, and other machine tools. According to the late Aubrey Williams (1880-1969), son of Walter Williams, a Great Western Iron & Steel Company corporate officer—Aubrey Williams had also been a watchman as a young man at the inactive facility around the turn of the century—Seattle's Moran Brothers Shipyards and Hofius & Pigott companies purchased most of the equipment. Williams said Moran was expanding prior to constructing the USS Nebraska (BB-14), a pre-dreadnaught US Navy battleship launched in Seattle in 1904. Hofius & Pigott was a steel firm owned by W.D. Hofius and William Pigott. In 1901, Pigott left the partnership and went on to form two of the area's great industrial ventures: Seattle Steel Company (later Bethlehem Steel Company) and Pacific Car and Foundry Company (later known as PACCAR).

The site of Houghton Beach Park in 1909. A steamer dock was located along the shore, and across the lake the Seattle side was virtually undeveloped. Some have identified the steamer as the *Fortuna*, but author Matt McCauley believes it is the *Urania*, which was dedicated to Kirkland-area service, whereas the *Fortuna* operated primarily on the Leschi-Mercer Island/Bellevue routes.

Ironically, Houghton resembles the 1909 scene more today than it has in the past decades. Thanks to the Houghton Beach Park purchase and the oil storage tank removal, in the 1960s, the neighborhood lost much of its World War II-era industrial appearance.

Despite the peaceful scene of the steamer landing at today's Houghton Beach Park, 1909 was a busy year in Houghton. Captain John Anderson had just become controlling partner at the shipyards—where Carillon Point now stands—and the Alaska-Yukon Pacific Exposition (AYPE), held across the lake, brought hordes of tourists to the region.

Before the floating bridges connected the Eastside to Seattle, residents depended on steam boats. Exposition tourism increased lake traffic, as Anderson built several elegant excursion steamers to accommodate the boom.

The roadway visible in the center of the old photo became Lake Washington Boulevard. The shoreline was closer to the road then, before the lake was lowered nine feet in 1916 with the opening of the Lake Washington Ship Canal.

The Lake House, a small hotel that served weary travelers from such far away hamlets as Redmond and North Bend, is on the left in the photo on page 26. It was demolished in the 1980s, when a modern building was erected at the site. The two small structures at the far right—then Houghton Post Office and a grocery store—still stand today.

Members of Kirkland's Barrie family enjoy an afternoon on the stern of the *Urania*.

The landing for the AYPE in 1909. It was for this international exposition that John Anderson increased his Lake Washington fleet. Most Kirkland residents made a point of traveling across the lake to visit the huge event.

27

1909, facing east on Union Bay during the AYPE. The busy waters off the University of Washington boathouse show chugging steamers dropping and fetching Exposition attendees.

A view from the deck of a steamer approaching Houghton in the same period of time. The two structures in the center, a grocery store and the Houghton Post Office, still stand today.

Kirkland *in* 1901: A Boomtown Gone Bust

Kirkland waterfront, about 1900. The photo looks east, where Kirkland Avenue, then Redmond Road, is just visible.

Eight years after the 1893 financial panic obliterated local hopes that Kirkland would become a great industrial center, Kirklanders were a mixture of pre-boom settlers and people who, lured here in the late 1880s and early 1890s by the promise of Peter Kirk's steel mill, stayed on after its failure.

Kirkland suffered from a shortage of developers in 1901. It needed investment and industry, and lacking these, it was financially depressed. Only a fraction of the structures and roads planned in the 1880s were built, so Kirkland was a hodgepodge of neglected and isolated buildings.

The photo above depicts what many said would be Kirkland's salvation—the ferry dock at the end of Kirkland Avenue. King County established a ferry run from Madison Park to Kirkland in 1900, so travelers had to pass through Kirkland. As a result, a few small businesses sprang up to serve the ferry passengers.

The photo faces east, and Kirkland Avenue—the road winding from the dock and over the hill—went all the way to Redmond. The lake level was nine feet higher then, and the road built on pilings, running in front to the Kirkland Livery and Feed Stable, became Lake Street South.

Most of the water in the foreground covers what later became Marina Park. The wharfing is an impressive accomplishment, considering there was no pile driver on the lake in the early 1900s.

Unfortunately, the ferry brought little revenue into town and the county-subsidized competition hurt several Houghton residents who operated small, private steamboats on the lake. Ironically, those same Houghton boat builders established a shipyard which became the area's major industry for several decades.

This view is to the south, along Lake Street South. The lake comes to the street and the ferry slip is visible at the right.

During the economic slump of the early years of the 1900s, many Kirkland residents abandoned the town and moved away. The real estate firm Burke & Farrar, which purchased the real estate previously owned by the old Kirkland Land & Improvement Company, took out newspaper ads in an effort to protect the value of its own extensive holdings in town.

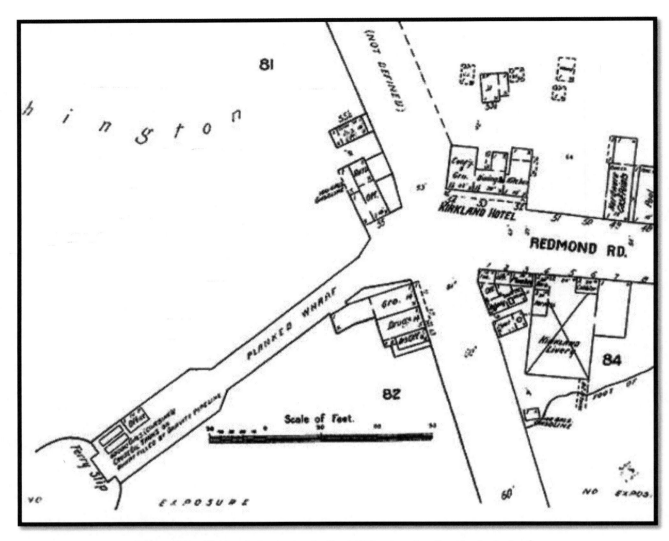

A plan of the Kirkland city center, in the 1890s, showing the planked wharf.

FIRST DEGREE MURDER CHARGE IS FILED AGAINST H. H. LOY

Kirkland jeweler Harry Loy

On the morning of July 28, 1931, Louis "Louie" Todd, owner of Todd's Feed Store, left his store carrying a package to the nearby bank. He ran into Harry H. Loy in front of Loy's jewelry store. The two men exchanged words; Loy was excited and accusatory, while Todd was calm and reassuring. Loy suddenly drew an automatic pistol and shot two bullets into Todd. Loy tried to keep firing, but his gun jammed.

Bystanders carried Todd, mortally wounded, back into his feed store and eased him into the chair at his desk. When the police arrived Loy told them, "If my gun hadn't jammed I'd be shooting yet!" The subsequent murder trial detailed one of the strangest shootings in Kirkland's history.

Prosecutors argued Loy's actions were premeditated murder, but Loy claimed the shooting was justified as an act of self defense, and that he was protecting his home and family. Loy and other witnesses testified Todd, who was married, paid "unwelcome attentions" to Loy's wife, Marie Loy. They said Todd visited Marie Loy at her home several times, while Harry Loy was gone. And on another occasion, they said he "followed her" to a resort cabin at North Beach. Even worse, Marie Loy said Todd had touched her hip.

Loy was incensed. He wrote vicious letters to Todd, calling him a "yellow viper" and a "cur," threatening to counteract Todd's "black hearted adulterous design."

At his trial, Loy defended himself by saying he was simply warning Todd when he met him on the street. He said he knew Todd carried a gun and thought he was reaching for it, and to defend himself, drawing his own only after a "satanic scowl" crossed Todd's face.

Loy's testimony contradicted statements he gave the police immediately after the shooting, in which he admitted he waited for Todd to go to the bank that morning.

The nine-man, three-woman jury—convinced that Todd had pursued Loy's wife—said that was enough for them. They found the shooting justified "on the grounds of the unwritten law." Loy left the courthouse a free man and celebrated with friends and family late into the night.

In 1931 Todd was fatally shot by Kirkland jeweler Harry Loy, a homicide that became an area sensation. Louie Todd's feed company was located on today's Park Lane. Todd's building stands today at 120 Park Lane, and is occupied by the Howard/Mandville Gallery, Lai-Thai, and Ristorante Paradiso.

Loy, in his shop, serving a customer.

The victim Louie Todd was interred in the Kirkland Cemetery, in a grave that was never marked.

The shooter, Harry Loy, went free after a jury found him not guilty.

Todd's wife is flanked by their daughters. The picture was taken during the Loy trial.

Will They Decide Slayer's Fate?

THE WIFE—Mrs. Marie Loy, whose husband, Harry H. Loy, shot his friend and fellow townsman, Louis D. Todd.

THE WIDOW—Mrs. Louis D. Todd, who has asserted her belief that her husband was innocent of misconduct with Mrs. Loy.

Mrs. Loy and Mrs. Todd

Louie Todd ran weekly ads for Todd Feed Co. in the East Side Journal newspaper. Todd regularly wrote his own thought-provoking, unconventional ad copy to promote his business. This was the last to appear before Loy killed him.

35

In the bucolic Kirkland of the 1920s and early 1930s, the Todd Feed Co. sign was a prominent feature, upper right.

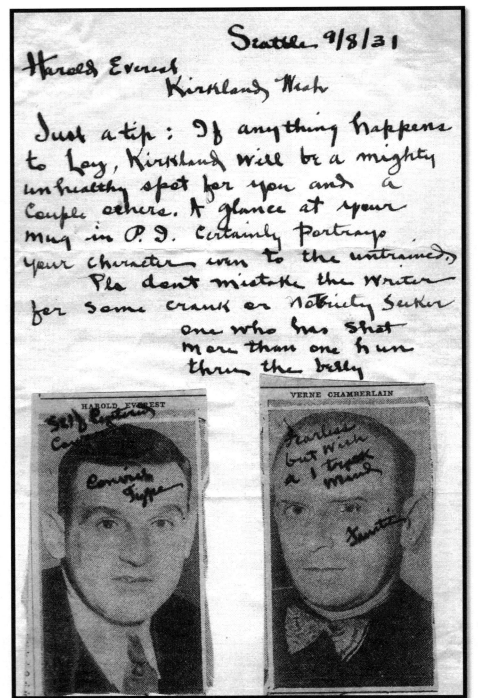

Seattle 9/8/31

Harold Everest
  Kirkland, Wash

Just a tip: If anything happens to Loy, Kirkland will be a mighty unhealthy spot for you and a couple others. A glance at your mug in P.I. certainly portrays your character even to the untrained.
  Pls dont mistake the writer for some crank or notriety seeker one who has shot more than one hun thru the belly

HAROLD EVEREST

VERNE CHAMBERLAIN

After Loy's acquittal most Kirkland citizens were outraged at what they perceived to be a miscarriage of justice. A committee, headed by *East Side Journal* publisher H.P. "Dick" Everest (1893-1967) formed to persuade Loy to leave town. Most people from outside Kirkland supported these efforts, but some did not, as evidenced by death threats like the one to the left. However, supporting letters like the one to the next page outnumbered the death threats.

Death threat, addressed to East Side Journal publisher H.P. "Dick" Everest.

Here an anti-Semitic supporter of the 'Businessmen's Committee' offers a new slogan for the town: "Kirkland for your MURDERS." It never caught on.

Longview, Washington.
October, 7th, 1931.

Mr. Harold Everest, et al,
Publisher,
Kirkland, Washington.

Gentlemen:

Congratulations on the stand you have taken in the Loy matter. It shows the world that Kirkland is still worthy to stay on the map. But what a package to hand some other community.

As the old Jew said " Between me, and between you " the first murder I commit I shall bring my victim to Kirkland.

Very truly yours,

P.S. Just in case you boys should fail in this matter might I suggest a slogan for Kirkland.
"Kirkland for your MURDERS"

1888: Settlers, Peter Kirk, and the Bank Building

A very early view of the Bank Building, prior to Market Street's construction. The wooden structures to the left were built by Andrew Nelson as part of his homestead. Since the lake was then nine feet higher, much of today's Marina Park is still lake bottom in this shot.

If you're going to build a steel manufacturing empire, you need an office. If that empire is on a lake, you also need a dock. Worry about the rest later. Judging from the 1888 photo, and in retrospect, that seems to have been Peter Kirk's plan.

Before the Kirk investor group came along, most of today's downtown area comprised the Nelson and DeMott homesteads. Eastside activity centered in Houghton—then boasting churches, a hotel, a school and a road to Redmond. Thus, at the time the Nelson and DeMott properties comprised the outskirts of the settled areas.

The Kirk group, unable to purchase waterfront land from stubborn Houghton settlers, decided instead to build their mill and town on the Nelson and DeMott properties. They bought the land and began building immediately; they erected a brick works on a stream near Third Street.

Kirk moved into the Nelson house, just behind the barn in the old photo. As soon as the brick works was finished, the partners built the small building called the bank building, seen in the center. Located at the corner of today's Market Street and Central Way, where the GTE (Frontier, as of 2010) Building now stands, it became the headquarters of the investment venture.

Demolished in the 1950's, many longtime Kirklanders well remember the structure. Bricks made at the brick works were later used to build the remaining Kirk-era buildings at the intersection of market Street and Seventh Avenue.

The dock was a necessary early project, to accommodate boomtown-bound passengers and freight from Seattle.

Because the lake was nine feet higher today than then, the dock was at the foot of where Market Street is now. Now the land slopes down into Marina Park, but at the time it was under water. Kirk called that inlet Moss Bay after a similar water feature near his home in England.

The higher water reached all the way to Lake Street South with a shallow, swampy pond extending to Peter Kirk Park, making the area a much more pronounced bay at that time.

The same view after Market Street was cut through. The structures at the wharf were warehouses but became Kirkland's first city hall and jail.

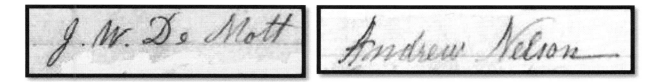

Pioneer Andrew Nelson's homestead claim comprised much of today's downtown Kirkland. Moss Bay was previously called Nelson Bay, after him.

A freight bag addressed to L. H. Marsh (Ludwig "Lute" Marsh) DeMott's Landing." John DeMott was a pre-Kirk settler. The above bag was provided by Jerry Marsh, Ludwig's grandson. Jerry Marsh's uncle, Ludwig's son, Louis Marsh, was an early Boeing business leader. He built Kirkland's Marsh Mansion. The Marsh family came to Kirkland in 1905.

Looking northwest, across Moss Bay. The old shoreline is clearly visible

View north, looking up Market Street before 1900. The two steamers at the Kirkland Lumber and Manufacturing Company wharf are probably the *Gazelle*, left, and the *Success*, right.

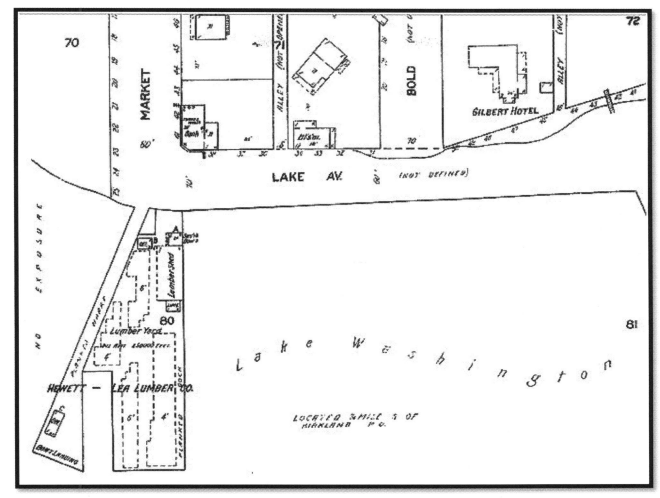

A drawing of part of the Kirkland waterfront, 1912.

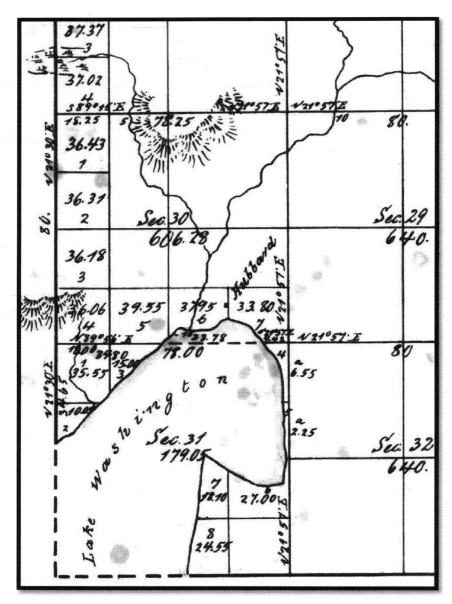

The Juanita area was surveyed in 1855, 1859, and again in 1870 for the General Land Office. At that time logger Martin Hubbard had the sole dwelling on Juanita Bay. Henry Goldmyer, also a logger, had a homestead claim at the eastern edge of the bay and the southwest portion of Section 29, but no structure was erected by the time of the 1870 survey. Goldmyer, 26, drowned in the Sammamish Slough in 1877 when he slipped and hit his head while on a raft of logs floating downstream. A decade later, Hubbard would also slip off a log raft and drown in Lake Washington, near Rose Point. Goldmyer's brother, William, was Sand Point's first homesteader and Goldmyer Hot Springs, near North Bend, is named for him.

Juanita has had several names over the years. The Eastside's earliest residents considered the land near the broad, shallow bay some of the most desirable along the Lake Washington shore. One of Juanita's earliest names was Tubtubiux, with was the name of a Sammamish village. The Sammamish people lived mostly in the Sammamish River Valley and had legends that reach back 12,000 years, when the lake was still part of Puget Sound.

Juanita Bay's abundance of food lured them to the Eastside. There were freshwater clams, crayfish, water chestnuts and wapato—a potato-like bulb —as well as fish and game that flourished in the shallows. Early trappers and explorers (from the 1830s) unwittingly brought diseases, such as smallpox, which decimated the Sammamish and other Native Americans on the Eastside.

Juanita's first permanent white settler was either Martin Hubbard or Henry Goldmyer, both loggers and 19 or 20 years of age when they established their land claims on the bay in 1870. Goldmyer's claim ran along the eastern edge of the bay. He erected a crude landing at about the foot of today's N.E. 116th Street. In the 1880s the post office knew the place as Hubbard, though the name Juanita was in common informal use at least as far back as 1872. Goldmyer drowned in May, 1877 when he slipped and hit his head as he fell off a raft of logs floating down the Sammamish River, then called the Squak Slough. He was 26.

Hubbard's next neighbors came in 1877. Dorr Forbes, a Civil War veteran, and Eliza Forbes moved west from Iowa, and built a cabin at what became N.E. 116th Street and 100th Ave. N.E. In 1882 they owned land on Rose Hill, near Forbes Lake, and tried growing cranberries there. Beavers won the battle for the possession of the lake, so they sold that claim and built a shingle mill on Juanita Creek. The Rowland Langdon and Charles Dunlap families came later in 1877 and settled farther up N.E. 116th.

Martin Hubbard drowned in the lake in 1887 after he slipped, like Goldmyer, off of a raft of boom sticks (logs). Prior to that, the nascent settlement of Hubbard had become Juanita, named after a popular song of the day. Juanita Dunlap was the first white child born in the area. Her family lived on the south side of N.E. 116th, east of the 108th Ave. N.E. The Langdons lived across N.E. 116th, the present location of McAuliffe Park.

Rowland Langdon built his house about 1887, and later his son Harry built a house next door. In 1902, Harry opened Juanita Grocery at the foot of N.E. 116th, which was known for years as both R. Langdon Road and King County Road Number 33. In fact, the original petition to create the road was filed in 1872 by Hubbard, Goldmyer, and John Steeves, whose claim was east, on the Sammamish Slough. Near the turn of century the Julius Ostberg family bought the Langdon's acreage. The late Joanne McAuliffe, an Ostberg descendant, lived on the property where she and her husband, Jerry McAuliffe, operated McAuliffe's Nursery from 1957 until 2001. The family sold the land to the City of Kirkland for McAuliffe Park in 2001.

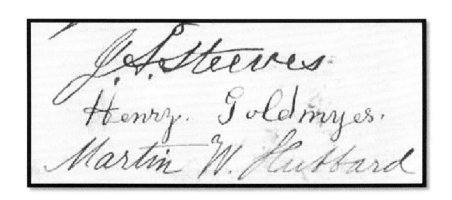

Juanita settler Martin Hubbard drowned in an 1887 logging accident.

Rowland Langdon (1818-1907) built this house on his homestead in 1887. The Ostberg family bought most of his claim in 1903. Ostberg descendants, the Johnson and McAuliffe families, remained continuously on the property until they sold it to the City of Kirkland for McAuliffe Park, in 2001. Young Alice (Ostberg) Johnson (1905 – 1983) sits with her dog on the front porch in the late 1900s.

Harry Langdon was a Juanita entrepreneur. He was a logger, a grocer, and the owner of the first repair shop for motorized vehicles in the area. His grocery store was on the N.E. corner of the intersection of N.E. 116th Street and 98th Avenue N.E., then known as Juanita Junction. Langdon was well-known for his big heart. Often, against his business' best interests, he extended credit for groceries to families during hard economic times, especially families with children. Ultimately, this led to the insolvency of his grocery store, shortly before his death in 1927.

Juanita Grocery

Harry Langdon, Prop..

GENERAL MDSE.

Good Goods at right Prices.   Prompt delivery.
Phone us your orders.   Ind. A 54.

Harry Langdon at his Juanita Junction auto shop with his early logging truck—note the wood-spoke wheels and solid rubber tires. His shop was located at the S.W. corner of the intersection of N.E. 116th Street and 98th Avenue N.E.

View of Juanita Bay's old shoreline, looking southeast from the first Juanita bridge. This area is now dry land that 98th Avenue N.E. cuts through.

Juanita Junction in the 1920s, view looking east up N.E. 116th Street. The parked cars belong to Juanita Beach patrons. Harry Langdon's store and garage are visible in the background.

Harry Langdon feeds his chickens at Juanita Junction. N.E. 116th Street, then called Langdon Road, left, leads up Little Finn Hill.

1923: The 'new' Union 'A' High School at Kirkland.

The Union 'A' High School at Kirkland.

Although Kirkland's Union 'A' High School is gone, its memory remains etched in many senior Kirklanders' minds and hearts. The first class graduated in 1923. Before that, local students attended either Kirkland High School at the old Central School location—the present site of city hall—or they rode the ferry to attend schools in Seattle.

Roughly 25 students graduated on June 14, 1923. R. E. Storey was the principal. The football team—en route to an undefeated regular season—beat Tolt, Issaquah, Bothell, North Bend, and tied Snoqualmie. Unfortunately, Auburn beat them in the championship playoffs.

The school colors were purple and white, and the school play that year was *Green Stockings*.

The Union 'A' School system predated the Lake Washington School District and students came from neighboring communities: Kirkland (Central), Juanita, Rose Hill, Houghton, and Bellevue's Northup and Points areas.

The late Juanita native Dorris (Forbes) Beecher, class of '32, said students from outside Kirkland were careful to call the school Union 'A' High School in Kirkland rather than "Kirkland High School."

The late Donald Barrie, class of 1928, said the school offered both vocational and college curricula, allowing students to develop skills matching their future career goals. His wife, the late Mabel Barrie, class of 1931, said academic requirements were rigorous by today's standards. She said she studied both Spanish and Latin, in addition to advanced math and chemistry. Mabel went on to the University of Washington as did many of her classmates. Much like other Finnish-speaking students who were to win awards in debate and oration and then graduate Union 'A' High School, she learned English in elementary school from non-Finnish speaking teachers and classmates.

From 1945, the school was renamed Lake Washington High School. After the current Lake Washington High School building opened in 1950, the Union 'A' "Terrace Hall" building became a part of the Kirkland Junior High complex. A dramatic fire destroyed the building on May 16, 1973, marking the end of 50 years of service to Kirkland's kids.

Clearing the land, in 1919, in preparation for the construction of the Union 'A' High School.

Jerry Marsh, Class of '41. His family came to Kirkland on July 3, 1905.

A track-meet event at Union 'A' High School.

Jewell Rasmussen, Class of '41. "To be gentle is the test of a lady" was her senior quote.

Chemistry class, 1940-41 school year.

After serving as a part of the Kirkland Junior High complex, the old Union 'A' building burned on May 16, 1973.

1892: The Barefoot Boy at the Old Langdon School

The 1893 class of the old Langdon Road School in Juanita.

The Langdon Road School operated from 1892 until 1916. Taken in 1893, the above photo shows Juanita-area children in front of the school. It must have been a special occasion, inasmuch as wreaths hang above the entrance. Some of the early families represented are Forbes, Spinney, Alexander, Dunlap, Josten, Longdon, Wittenmyer, Smith, and Daniels. The teacher was Sarah Foley.

The one-room schoolhouse classically symbolizes 19th century western frontier community values and strengths. These schools evoke images of morning flag salutes, ink wells in the wooden desks, lunches in lard pails, writing slates, and immortalized maxims such as: "I used to walk to school barefoot, three miles in the snow."

Juanita area youngsters originally attended school in a log structure located on the Dunlap property, off N.E. 116th (Langdon Road), behind today's A.G. Bell Elementary. In 1892, the residents built the clapboard school—shown in the above photo—on the north side of N.E. 116th St. at about 111th Ave. N.E.

The students in the 1893 photo were some of the first white children born in the Juanita area, the offspring if the area's early settlers. For these kids, dinner at home was often venison and stinging nettles served like spinach. Juanita families lived off the land more than the steel mill crowd over in Kirkland, so the financial panic that year didn't affect Juanita as much.

The Wittenmyer family lived near today's Totem Lake Mall, which was built in the early 1970s. Since then, people have called the small lake there Totem Lake, but mall developers fabricated that name. Many senior Kirklanders still use its original name: Lake Wittenmyer, or Mud Lake.

The seven-year-old barefoot boy in the front row is Lloyd Leslie Forbes, who was called Les. His mother Eliza sent him to school wearing shoes every day, but en route would take them off, hiding them in the bushes. The photographic evidence caught him in the act and no doubt there was a scolding in future. Years later he established Juanita Beach with his wife Alicia (Stuart) Forbes.

Myth is often based in fact. Some of these children *did* walk miles to school in snow. Young Les *did* make the trek barefoot, at least until Mrs. Forbes saw the photo.

The old Langdon Road School in Juanita operated from 1892 until 1916. The photo was probably taken at about the turn of the century.

William Shannon (1876-1976) was the teacher at the old Langdon Road Juanita Elementary School teacher in 1903. Shannon was a civil engineer who supervised the construction of the Baker River Dam and hydro power plant near Concrete, WA, and the Shuffleton steam plant in Renton. The Baker River Dam created Lake Shannon, named in his honor.

The second Central School, seen here in 1905, was located on the site where Kirkland City Hall stands today.

By 1890, Kirkland was a growing town, attracting more and more new residents. Many newcomers drawn to the steel mill boom town had young children in tow. Unfortunately, those who bought homes from Peter Kirk's company found the closest school for their kids was down in Houghton. In those days, the journey from Kirkland to Houghton was a time consuming trek across a waterfront road made of muddy, split logs.

Besides, no one in Kirkland wanted to rely on Houghton. Kirkland was to be a great metropolis, so the solution was simple: they built a school in Kirkland. Constructed in 1890, the first Central School was a one room structure, located on the southeast corner of First Street and Fifth Avenue, where the Kirkland City Hall parking lot stands today. It offered both elementary and high school grade levels.

The first school weathered the changes in Kirkland's fortunes, from boom to bust. It was originally intended as a temporary facility, but the 1893 financial crash reduced the stream of new residents to a trickle, so a new school building had to wait.

In 1904, J. G. Bartsch built the second Central School, shown in the 1905 photo (above). Bartsch also built an elementary school on Rose Hill a few years later. (He should not be confused with his son, Captain George Bartsch, an early Houghton shipbuilder and shipyard co-owner.)

Like the first Central School, the second offered both elementary and high school grades. There were two grades in each classroom, with the elementary on the first level and the high school upstairs, After 1923, when the new high school was built on Waverly Way, the Central School continued as an elementary school. Many senior Kirklanders attended classes in the structure before it was razed in 1935.

The final Central School, built in 1935 on the same site was partially funded by the Works Progress Administration (also known as the WPA). That Central School served students until 1969, after which it was used as a teaching support facility. The City of Kirkland eventually built the current city hall on the site which had served so many generations of Kirkland kids.

Students at the original Central School in 1897. The teacher was William Boggs.

A rare interior view of the second Central School.

Kirkland builder J. G. Bartsch constructed the second Central School in 1904.

Kirkland's high school football team, 1914.

Taken a little after 1905, from a glass negative, probably by Mattie Schuster of the Marsh family.

The third Central School was built in 1935.

The third Central School, shortly before demolition.

Students from the first school at Houghton, seen in the 1880s. The O'Conner children are identified. A partially logged Yarrow Point is in the background.

Life in the Washington Territory settlement of Pleasant Bay was tough in the 1870s and 1880s. Although most who settled there (the name would later become Houghton) came west by train, they endured similar hardships to those who came earlier by covered wagon, as they carved a community out of the thick, dark forest along the lakeshore.

Other settlements in the region at that time centered on coal mining, logging, and sawmills. Without such industrial concentrations Houghton had much less of the drunkenness, violence, and vice that such communities experienced.

During a decade in which gunfights ruled in many towns, the Pleasant Bay community contained a proportionately large number of women whose presence exerted a civilizing influence on the rough and tumble frontier. At a ratio of one woman to five men, Pleasant Bay was way ahead of most of the territory. There were no saloons or gambling houses, and few shootings. Churches and a school sprang up.

The first school was located across from today's Marsh Park on Lake Washington Boulevard. Harry

French, a settler who arrived and built a primitive cabin in 1872, moved into a frame house in 1874 and then donated his cabin to the community for use as a schoolhouse. The desks and seats were crudely made of split logs. The first teacher was William Easter, a carpenter who was unemployed during the winter, which allowed him time to teach.

In those days, completing the eighth grade was an impressive accomplishment. The school year was shorter than it is today. The older students had to help out on parent's homesteads. Many students carried firearms to school, in case they encountered game on their way home.

The photo below depicts many of children of Houghton's first families, including the DeMotts, the Churches, and the Nelsons. The O'Conner children are labeled. Sadly, death from accidents and diseases prevented several kids in the photo from reaching adulthood.

The man located in the center of this photo of Houghton-area school children is William Easter, the first teacher. Easter was the first settler to claim a homestead at Eagle Point, later changed to Yarrow Point, and he also took passengers back and forth to Madison Park in his small sailboat. When the wind died his passengers had to help paddle. Easter later constructed a small steamboat, the *Edith E.*, named to honor his wife.

1904: Juanita Elementary School

As Juanita entered the 20th century, new and growing families created the need for a large, modern schoolhouse. In 1904, Andrew Nelson built a two level structure on the southwest corner of what became N.E. 132nd St. and 100th Ave. N.E. He lived across N.E. 132nd, where Albertson's stands today.

Many Juanita schoolchildren were Finnish kids who lived on both Big and Little Finn Hills, with last names such as Turtainen, Pakala, and Mattila. The late Dorris (Forbes) Beecher and the late Mabel (Turtainen) Barrie were classmates at the school during the 1910s and 1920s. Both told stories of Finnish classmates who returned to Finland and Russia with their families. The women said their friends wrote letters regularly, but after the Communist Revolution and civil war the letters stopped coming. The decade of violence killed many.

Although the students were spread over a wide geographic area, there was transportation to school. Anna Ostberg, the school cook, carted kids around in a horse drawn buckboard. Later, Mr. Tapp and Ed Watson drove the students in a Ford Model T bus.

The school building was expanded twice and a gym was also added. The above photo shows the school in its earliest configuration. Several of the group photos of the students were taken in front of the school during the late 1910s by the famous Pacific Northwest photographer Darius Kinsey.

One of the early principals was Edward Robinson. John Viele had the job from 1933, and he also taught full-time. In those days Juanita was School District 21. It didn't merge with Kirkland and Redmond until 1944.

In 1951, Juanita Elementary replaced the remodeled 1904 schoolhouse, which was torn down to make room for the ball field. The adjoining school caretaker's house was moved to a new location nearby and was owned for decades by the late Don and Mabel Barrie—it still stands today, and it remains one of the precious few surviving reminders of early school days on the Eastside.

A look inside the old Juanita Elementary School.

Juanita School District 21 enlarged the structure substantially.

100th Avenue N.E. has changed a little since this photo was made. Looking south, just south of the intersection at N.E. 132nd Street.

View facing east from the back of the school. The road at the left is N.E. 132nd St., which was named at different times East Road and Ed Langdon Road.

In its final configuration the school was substantially expanded and a gym added at the rear.

A view from the air, in 1949, facing west. The Juanita Community Center, located in the center of the photo, still stands today. The old Juanita School is seen at the right—the structure and attached gym. The old Manning Farm is at the left. The small home at the bottom still stands, surrounded by an apartment complex.

The present day Juanita Elementary School, located on the same property as the 1904 structure, pays homage to the past: it boasts a basketball court cover that is a replica of the historic building.

Pleasant Bay Becomes Houghton, and Some Families Therein: C. 1879

The top photo shows the old Houghton School after its stairs were remodeled. Houghton students, below, are seen with the original stairs.

In 1885, Judge E. Smith described Houghton in a letter a friend as "wild, primitive country." Even so, settlers then numbered about 100 and the Houghton School had replaced Harry French's small cabin, which settlers used as the first school structure there. The Houghton School stood across from Yarrow Bay at N.E. 52nd Street, then called Curtis Road after the Curtis family, another prominent early Houghton family.

Around 1879 the community changed its name from Pleasant Bay to Houghton. There are two stories about the origin of the name change. They are equally creditable, according to one Eastside history authority and Kirkland resident, Dr. Lorraine McConaghy. In the popular version, the name change honored the Houghtons, a generous Boston family who—wanting to help Christian people in the faraway Washington Territory—donated a bell to the First Church of Christ at Pleasant Bay, which today is Kirkland Congregational Church.

The Houghton family had a fine bell shipped from the east and the grateful citizens named the community Houghton. Kirkland Congregational Church still has that bell. The second, less colorful version holds that the community was named for loggers James and Willard Houghton, brothers who lived nearby. James' daughter Susie attended the Houghton School, and may be one of the young women in the photographs.

Two Northup boys are also pictured. The Northups owned large tracts of land south of Houghton at the southern end of Yarrow Bay, then called Northup Bay. Some of today's senior Kirklanders still remember Northup's Landing there.

For many years City of Bellevue street signs mistakenly read Northrup Way for the road named for the family, but most signs now display the more accurate Northup Way. The pioneering Mr. and Mrs. Northup rest in the Kirkland Cemetery.

(**2010 Update**: Since this column was published in 1993, Kirkland Heritage Society President Loita Hawkinson has unearthed information showing that the Pleasant Bay community first hoped to name its settlement Edison, but postal authorities blocked that idea because the name was already in use. Hawkinson also clearly establishes that the Houghton brothers came after the name had been selected to honor the Houghton family of Boston.)

"Wild, primitive country." An early view from Yarrow Point of the Curtis property, with house in the center-right, taken by Houghton pioneer Harry French prior to the construction of the Houghton School. The crude road leading into the thick forest on the right was called Curtis Road. It became N.E. 52nd Street.

A later view showing the Curtis home, Curtis Road and N.E. 52nd St, and the old Houghton School. Along the shoreline is a puncheon walkway (a puncheon is a piece of roughly dressed timber with one face finished flat).

The old Houghton School, shortly after its completion. Later photos show the entry stairs were remodeled.

1993: Documenting Kirkland's Past.

Seen at Marina Park in 1969, the late Arline Stokes (then an *East Side Journal* reporter who later published material as Arline Ely and Arline André) interviews Lancelot "Lanny" Ross (1906-88). Ross was a popular singer, radio entertainer and film star from the 1930s through the 1950s, whose grandfather, Walter Williams, came to Kirkland from Workington, England. There Williams had been secretary of Peter Kirk's Moss Bay Hematite Iron & Steel Company. In 1888 he was a co-founder of the Kirkland Land & Improvement Company and Moss Bay Iron & Steel company of America, with Peter Kirk, Seattle co-founder Arthur A. Denny, and other noted local financiers.

The City of Kirkland is taking its own "look to the past" and the result is a great source of historical data about the area. People sometimes ask where the information for this column comes from because they want to know more about a particular topic. Information comes from several sources.

The best place to start is with the only comprehensive history of Kirkland, *Our Foundering Fathers* by the late Arline Ely (she also wrote as Arline Stokes and later Arline André). Formerly an *East Side Journal* reporter, André wrote her book over seven years, finishing it in 1975. It is an entertaining history of Kirkland and much of her research involved interviews with early residents. A former Juanita resident and a mom of two daughters, from the 1960s she reported for *The East Side Journal* newspaper where she wrote frequently about Kirkland history.

Unfortunately, her book has been out of print for many years, but the Kirkland and Kingsgate libraries have copies. The Kirkland library has a shelf devoted to local history, but you have to ask about it at the desk.

Probably the most exciting source of information is the city-sponsored Kirkland history project, headed by Dr. Lorraine McConaghy. The project involves three areas: census data, indexing the old *East Side Journal,* and oral history. There are now over 10,000 entries in the *East Side Journal* database, thanks largely to Alan Stein, a project volunteer who has read and indexed nearly 15 years of back issues that date from 1918 to 1975. The paper started publication in 1918. It provides an interesting view of Kirkland's development.

For the oral history project, volunteers are taping interviews with area seniors. Oral history provides a highly personal view of the past and can often be more accurate than other sources.

The Kirkland Heritage Society is also devoted to preserving and recording Kirkland's history. It meets monthly and publishes historical information in its award-winning newsletter, *Blackberry Preserves*. For more info call KHS at (425) 827-3446.

OUR FOUNDERING FATHERS

Arline Ely

Now long out of print, *Our Foundering Fathers* is a comprehensive history of Kirkland that was published in 1975. It is reproduced online, at kirklandheritage.org. Its author spent seven years interviewing area seniors, scouring business records, journals, newspapers, and other primary sources to create a highly informed look at Kirkland's early days. Since 1975 the City of Kirkland has expanded its borders substantially through annexations, leaving many new areas of exploration for future researchers.

The Curtis Family of Houghton

James (1810-96), young Wilbur (1880-98), and Will Curtis (1840-1923), working on their homestead, about 1890. They were photographed by Walt Curtis (1874-1945).

While many early Eastside settlers came west by train, Houghton's Curtis family made the trek to Puget Sound in true pioneer fashion—by covered wagon. The family started their journey from their home in South Dakota. The parents, James and Sophia (1814-99), were nearly 60 years old when they arrived, accompanied by their grown children William, Frank (1842-1918), and Florell Northup (1853-1928).

They settled first in Seattle, then a small, rough-and-tumble logging town, where they lived for seven years. In the early 1870s they bought a large parcel of land on the lake, where Carillon Point stands today. In 1883, Frank and his wife, Molly (1846-1925), erected the second frame home in the Houghton area at the Curtis family compound.

There was an ancient trail that went eastward from the Curtis property, over the hill to the head of Lake Sammamish where Redmond now stands. The King County Commissioners selected the trail for development into a road in 1856, to connect the fertile hop growing Snoqualmie area with Lake Washington's shore.

The Civil War and other distractions deflected the road project, and it didn't get built until 1880. It was called Curtis Road and became an important link to Seattle for Redmond and Sammamish Valley settlers, who rode across the lake by steamboat from Curtis Landing.

Despite growing up in land-locked South Dakota, the Curtis men were steamboating pioneers. Frank served as engineer aboard the *Squak*, the first steamer built on the lake in 1885. When the boat sank in1890, the Curtis family sold a small section of land to finance their own boat, the *Elfin*. This venture provided capital to build a large dock in front of their home—Curtis Wharf—where they constructed their second steamer, the *Mist*.

Finding their property particularly well-suited to boat building, they built another boat, the *Peerless,* and sailed it out of Lake Washington on the Black River to operate on Puget Sound.

In 1901, they sold a section of their waterfront to Captains George Bartsch and Harry Tompkins, who were brothers-in-law. That sale and the development of a small commercial shipyard there would eventually have profound impact on the economic future of Houghton and Kirkland.

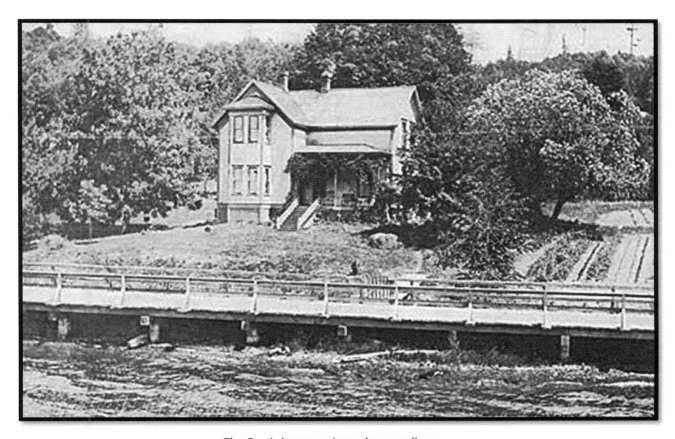

The Curtis home and puncheon walkway.

78

The Curtis family built the *Peerless* at their property in 1901. Taking her out of the lake by the Black River that spring proved an arduous task—the river level was low and the vessel became stuck in the shallows several times, and in fact it remained stuck for over five months before the winter rains raised the lake level enough to float the vessel out to Puget Sound.

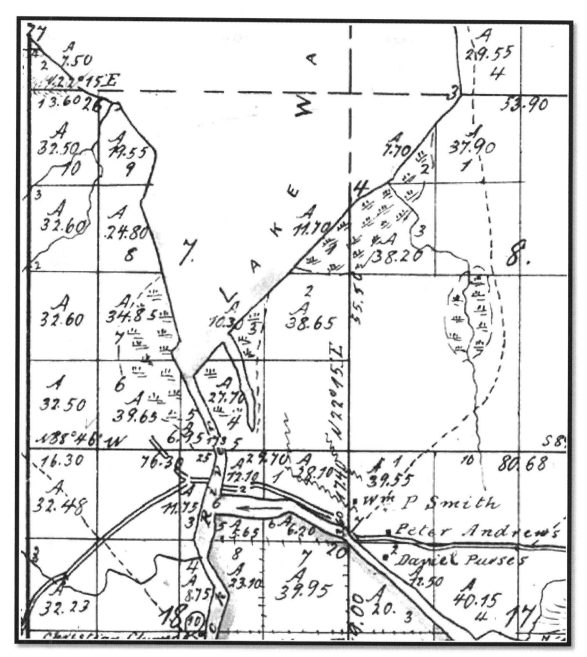

This government survey from 1865 shows today's Renton area where the old Black River drained Lake Washington and the confluence with Cedar River was south of the lake. These rivers eventually joined the Duwamish River, near today's Tukwila, and flowed into Puget Sound. With difficulty, during times of high water, it was possible to bring a boat into or out of the lake by these rivers. In 1916 the completion of the Lake Washington Ship Canal lowered the lake nine feet and the Black River dried up. The Cedar River was rerouted slightly to feed into the lake.

1865-1880s: Early Lake Washington Steamboating, Captain Jay C. O'Conner, and his Lura Maud.

Jay C. O'Conner as a young private in M Company of the 1st Wisconsin Heavy Artillery. He enlisted on August 29, 1864 at the age of 17. His battery was assigned to Washington, D.C. defenses at Forts Lyon, Weed, and Farnsworth.

To the first Eastside settlers, Lake Washington probably seemed like another barrier to progress. The eastern shore of the lake gave access to the salt-water port and growing town of Seattle, and contact with civilization, and on the lake's eastern shore was the promise of fortune to be made in natural resources such as coal and timber. The main problem was how to connect the Eastside to Seattle.

Writing in 1934, R. H. Collins, Kirkland's first mayor, said of the early days, "Separated from Seattle as we are by Lake Washington, transportation has always been a vital problem in the development of this section."

Canoes and rowboats were the first transport on the lake, but when coal was discovered at Newcastle (south of Bellevue), steamboats became a necessity, for towing coal-laden barges to the Seattle side. In 1868, *Fannie*—the first powered craft on the lake—appeared. In those days, lake level was nine feet higher than it is today (the Lake Washington ship canal would not connect the lake to Puget Sound until 1916).

At the south end of the lake, the Black River drained out of the lake near where the Cedar River flows in today. The Black River joined with the White River, which then fed into the Duwamish River, which in turn flowed into Puget Sound.

During times of high water, it was possible to bring a boat from Puget Sound up the rivers and into the lake. The process took weeks and often involved winching the boat through the shallows and removing wind-felled trees from the river. Local Native Americans were often hired along the way to help. By the 1870s several other boats had made the arduous passage up the rivers. These boats towed coal barges and carried passengers across the lake.

To get to their new homesteads many of Kirkland's earliest settlers loaded all their belongings on these 40-65 foot vessels. One such pioneer was Juanita settler Eliza Forbes, who said in 1939 that the tiny vessel her family first rode across the lake in 1877 looked more like "a ship's boat" than a steamer because it was so small.

In the 1870s, Civil War veteran and early Houghton settler, Captain Jay C. O'Conner worked as a crewman aboard the coal-towing stern wheeler *Chehalis*. O'Conner learned a lot about boats and grew to know the lake well, later going on to operate some of the first boats on Lake Washington. He named his Houghton-built steamer *Lura Maud* after his daughters, Lura and Maud.

After it became practical to build boats on the lake in the 1880s the lake soon had a small fleet. As a result, fewer steamers made the time consuming and difficult trip through the river system.

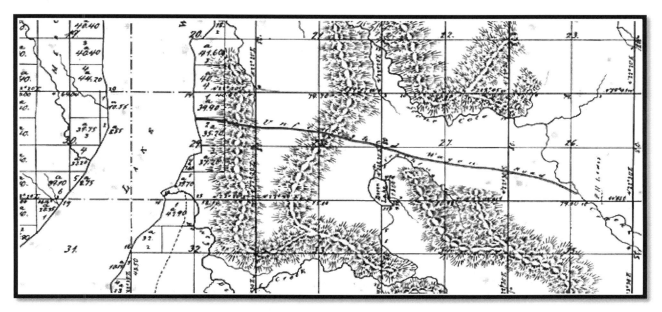

This 1864 government land survey shows Mercer Island, left, Lake Washington, and today's South Bellevue and Newcastle areas. The "Unfinished Wagon Road" led from the Newcastle coal mines to the lakeshore. Moving coal on barges encouraged the earliest Lake Washington steamboating efforts.

Jay C O'Conner's steamboat, the *Lura Maud*, was built on Lake Washington at Pontiac, immediately north of Sand Point, in 1887, by early settler and pioneer Lake Washington boat builder Edward Lee. The *Lura Maud* is probably the most misspelled boat name in the history of Lake Washington. It is often called the "Laura Maude," or other variations. Putting aside the fact that O'Conner's daughters were named "Lura" and "Maud" a magnified view of the name painted on the wheelhouse corrects the record.

Captain Jay C. O'Conner with Eve, his wife. The two lived north of the Curtis claim, south of the French family, and while Jay was operating various lake steamboats, Eve was proprietress of the Lake House, Kirkland's first hotel. The couple later sold the Lake House to the Fish family.

1901: Captains Bartsch & Tompkins and Their B&T Transportation Company

Captain George Bartsch was 73 when this photo was taken for the June/July/August 1946 issue of *East Side Magazine*. Bartsch is holding the first edition of *The Kirkland Press* from 1905, in which he was mentioned. Bartsch was born in 1873 in Wisconsin, and came to Houghton in 1889 with his family. That year he became Kirkland High School's first graduate. His father, J. G. Bartsch, was a builder who constructed many important early Kirkland buildings. George Bartsch had many professions over the years: steamboat captain, builder, commercial laundry operator, hotel manager, and the owner of the Pastime Café.

When Captains George Bartsch and Harry Tompkins bought a section of waterfront land for their boat yard from the Curtis family in 1901, they set a course for Houghton development that lasted until after World War II. The two men were already deeply rooted in the Eastside.

Bartsch's father, J. G. Bartsch, was a Kirkland builder who had numerous projects to his credit, including two Peter Kirk residences (his family home on Waverly Way and Deer Lodge on San Juan Island), the first Rose Hill Elementary School, the Shumway Mansion, and the second Central School.

Before John Tompkins' association with Bartsch, he opened a grocery store at the corner of 7th Street and Market Street in 1890.

Both Bartsch and Tompkins were experienced Lake Washington steamboaters by 1901. Bartsch captained the lake's first double-ender ferry, the *King County of Kent*, and he worked on other early steamers. Tompkins was well into a career that would span 48 years on the lake and Puget Sound.

Initially, their shipyard was a primitive 10-foot by 12-foot shanty. Their first payroll consisted of 12 men, and they had a horse and wagon. Their crew worked with personal tools. The shipyard's first boats were launched only during the flood season on the lake (prior to the 1916 locks connecting the lake to Puget Sound, Lake Washington's level had a natural variance of about five feet in height between the wet and dry seasons). The Bartsch and Tomkins team later invested in a mule-powered windlass and marine ways on which to build their boats, which accommodated vessels up to 125 feet long.

The Houghton road network at that time was nothing more than a few muddy trails, and most the workers walked or rode horses to work, tying their mounts to the yard hitching post.

In addition to vessel construction and repair, the two men operated boats on the lake under the B&T Transportation banner. They owned the *Emily Keller*, the *Gazelle,* and the *Dorothy*, and ran the *King County of Kent* between Kirkland and Madison Park for King County, for which B&T was paid $140 per month.

The company also owned the *Success*, a 50-foot steamboat built by early Whidbey Island settler Captain Coupe at Coupeville in 1868 and was later brought into the lake by the Black River. She foundered in deep water off of Madison Park during a 1907 storm, one of the few intact—as opposed to burned or scuttled—early steamers lying on the lake floor still awaiting discovery by divers.

Bartsch and Tompkins' *Gazelle* could carry up to 75 passengers and in her time was considered the fastest steamer on the lake.

B&T Transportation Co. owned the early propeller-driven steamboat *Success*. Though neither fast nor comfortable, her diminutive size allowed her to make the arduous passage into the lake from Puget Sound by way of the Black River. The *Success* sits on the lake floor—her resting place for more than a century.

This 1908 view of the boatyard shows preparations for the 1909 Alaska-Yukon Pacific Exposition. The steamer *L. T. Haas*, left, burned and sank in 1909 and at the right the Atlanta Park dance pavilion is seen under construction. It was used for parties and entertainment, but eventually became a floating shop. This entire area is now a part of the Carillon Point development.

Emma (Bartsch) Tompkins was George Bartch's sister and George Tomkins' wife.

Captain George Bartsch's father, J. G. Bartsch (1840-1918), was a highly regarded Kirkland builder and hardware store owner. Seen here in front of his hardware store, located lakefront at the foot of Market Street, in the 1910s.

Kirkland Hardware Store

Keeps Wire Fencing, Poultry Net-ting, Building, Felt and Roofing Paper, Glass, Paint, Oil, Varnish, Stains and Paint Brushes, Down Spouts and Tin.

Everything at Low Prices

J. G. BARTSCH,   Prop.

This advertisement is from the July 7, 1911 issue of *The East Side News*.

1930: The Great O.L. "Deep" Higginbotham and Kirkland Baseball

An early 1930s team photo of the "Kirkland K-9," the town baseball team. O.L. "Deep" Higginbotham is kneeling, second player from the left. The photo was taken at the old baseball field off Waverly Way, where the former Union "A" High and the (1932) Kirkland Junior High schools stood—the site of today's Heritage Park.

My baseball team, the Mets, won the Kirkland Little League Championship in 1974, when I was 10. After our victorious game, I approached a group of four men—who were probably in their 60s— and asked them why they always watched our games even though they weren't related to any of our players.

The men laughed and said they just liked to watch baseball. They were all long-time Kirklanders, and they told me about previous decades, when Kirkland was a baseball-crazed town. They spoke of the large crowds that turned out to see the Kirkland semi-pro team, one of the city's main attractions, and they reminisced about all the old time players.

One name stayed in my memory, O.L. "Deep" Higginbotham, the man who played semi-pro ball on the Eastside for 28 years. At 90, not only is Higginbotham still around, he is more than willing to share his memories of a baseball career that began shortly after his family moved to Juanita in 1919.

When he started playing, Juanita had its own team. The men played home games on a crude diamond on the Ostberg property, now McAuliffe Park. Kirkland's team, on the other hand, played on the field off of Waverly Way but moved to the Peter Kirk Park site around 1939.

Higginbotham says that large crowds gathered on Sundays to watch the games, and Kirklanders would often pass a hat for donations to cover the visiting team's meals and traveling expenses. With Kirkland's reputation at stake, some fans offered our players money, $5 for a hit and $10 for a home run. That was pretty big money in those days.

Higginbotham usually played shortstop and batted leadoff. His lifetime batting average was over .300. His uncle, Irv Higginbotham, pitched for the Kirkland K-nine occasionally. He played pro ball for the St. Louis Cardinals and Chicago Cubs from 1906 to 1909.

Baseball didn't pay much, so Deep Higginbotham worked for Matzen Woolen Mill and other Kirkland businesses. He retired from baseball 1948, but still has his appointment book pasted with news clippings about team exploits over the years.

Higginbotham and his wife, Kirkland native Florence (Peterson) Higginbotham, recently celebrated their 65th wedding anniversary. The recollections of both Higginbothams are fascinating and deep; in fact, and just about the only thing he can't remember is how he got the nickname "Deep."

Irv Higginbotham (1881-1959) played pro baseball in the 1900s and greatly influenced his nephew, Deep Higginbotham. Irv spent the 1907 season in the minors, playing for the Northwestern League's Aberdeen (WA) Black Cats. The following season he was back in the majors, playing for the St. Louis Cardinals. Irv Higginbotham ended his career after the 1916 season, playing in the Western League for the Des Moines (Iowa) Boosters. Irv was a 6' 1", 196 pound pitcher.

During the 1920s Juanita's Ostberg family had a baseball diamond on their property and hosted games for the Juanita team. Mrs. Ostberg cooked chicken dinners, offered for sale to fans. The Ostberg property is the site of today's McAuliffe Park at 108th Ave N.E. and N.E. 116th Street—then called "Langdon Road." The baseball site is detailed below in the late Ruth Nelson's "Juanita: A 'Remember When' Map, drawn during the 1970s.

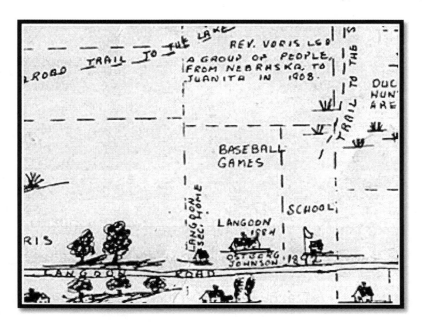

The Juanita Baseball Team, 1918.

Lucile McDonald and Early Reporting on Eastside History

The intersection of Lake Street South and Kirkland Avenue is seen in this 1920s photo from *Lucile McDonald's Eastside Notebook: 101 Local History Vignettes*.

One of the first journalists to write regularly about Eastside history was the late Lucile McDonald (1998-1992), shown in the photo at left. Marymoor Museum has recently published a collection of her best columns in: *Lucile McDonald's Eastside Notebook: 101 Local History Vignettes.*

Born in 1898, McDonald began her career in journalism during World War I, after attending the University of Oregon. McDonald and her husband settled in the Seattle area in the 1940s. There, she wrote for local papers and published children's fiction and other work. In the 1950s she began publishing regular local history feature columns and books. Her special interest was the Eastside and Lake Washington.

Her interviews with many of the area's settlers, who have long since passed from the scene, made her work popular. The idea for her book came from McDonald herself, shortly before her death in 1992. She discussed the project at length with the book's editor, Kirkland's own Dr. Lorraine

McConaghy, a recognized authority on Eastside history and development.

The work looks at the whole Eastside, and includes quite a bit about Kirkland, the first book to do so in nearly 20 years. For anyone interested in the Eastside's past, this book is a must have.

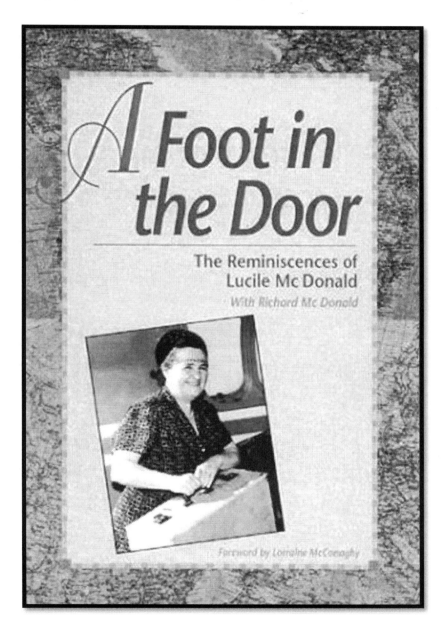

Lucile Saunders McDonald was a prolific writer who authored or co-authored 28 books and numerous newspaper columns and articles over a career that spanned seven decades. She wrote often of local history during her 23 years at the *Seattle Times Magazine* and in her weekly *Journal-American* newspaper column.

Captain John Anderson and his Freshwater Empire

Captain John Anderson (1868-1941) had more impact on Lake Washington transportation than any other person. He married Emilie Matson (1874-1959) in 1895. The two are seen here in 1911 with their prized Studebaker.

In 1888, a young Swedish immigrant seaman named John Anderson stepped off his ship in Seattle with $20 in his pocket. Though only 20, he had been at sea for six years and had just sailed around Cape Horn from the east coast. His decision to stay in Puget Sound would have a profound impact on the future of Kirkland.

With his nautical experience, Anderson quickly found a job as deckhand aboard the sleekest, fastest steamer then running on Lake Washington, the *C.C. Calkins*. He worked his way up the line of responsibilities, eventually sitting for his master's ticket and becoming Captain Anderson.

The *Calkins'* owners went bankrupt in 1893, but by then Anderson had saved enough money to buy his own steamer, the *Winnifred*. Anderson operated his boat all over Lake Washington and even up the Sammamish Slough into Lake Sammamish.

A shrewd businessman with big dreams, Anderson began buying and building lake steamers. He also bought lakefront property and built private parks on Mercer Island, Bellevue, and Houghton. His Houghton land, which adjoined the Bartsch and Tomkins boatyard, was called Atlanta Park.

In 1907, Anderson bought controlling interest in the yard and changed its name to the Anderson Shipyard. He also absorbed Bartsch and Tompkins' B&T Transportation Co. steamboat fleet and operated all the vessels under his Anderson Steamboat Company banner. With that, he virtually monopolized the Lake Washington water transportation industry.

He stepped up yard production, anticipating the Alaska-Yukon Pacific Exposition of 1909. He built several new steamers designed to carry excursion passengers to his lakeside parks in addition to regular passengers. He also increased the number of employees at his yard from 30 to 100, and spent more than $50,000 on capital improvements, including cranes and other equipment.

Anderson had 12 boats in service the summer of the AYPE, which benefited the Kirkland community by providing many jobs. In 1909, with a new canal and World War I just around the corner John Anderson was just getting warmed up.

John Anderson's first job on lake Washington was aboard the *C.C. Calkins*, a boat named for its owner built to serve as his ill-fated luxury hotel on the west shore of Mercer Island, then called East Seattle. The *Calkins* was the only Lake Washington steamboat that boasted a calliope.

Emilie (Matson) Anderson christens the *Aquilo* in 1909 at Houghton's Anderson Shipyard. The boat would operate under the Anderson Steamboat Company banner, as the logo on the bow indicates. John Anderson is at Emilie's right.

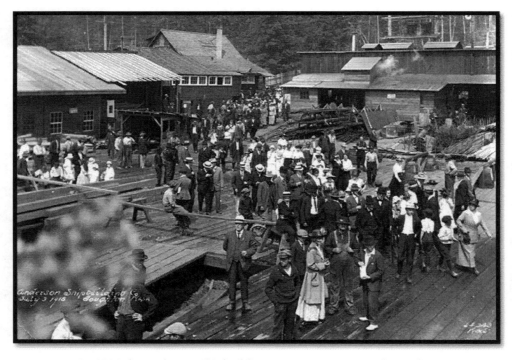

By 1918 the Anderson Shipbuilding Company was a very busy place.

This view from 1921 faces southeast. The wrecked lake steamer *Triton* is near the shore.

1920s: Ballinger Boat Works, the 'Other' Kirkland Shipyard

The 38-foot cabin-picket type patrol boats were used in harbors and similar protected waters. 538 were built, 68 at Ballinger. They had a single screw and topped out at about 25 knots.

Houghton wasn't the only Kirkland area shipyard involved in vessel construction during the early part of the 20th century. The other local shipyard was located on Lake Washington Boulevard, just north of 10th Avenue South, the old Kirkland-Houghton border.

Kirkland's yard began in the 1920s as Ballinger Boat Works. Many Kirkland seniors say the site was memorable because it was near two World War I cannons that used to guard the entrance to Kirkland, one on either side of Lake Washington Boulevard.

The Ballinger operation never approached the scale of the Lake Washington Shipyards at Houghton, though any local business that could support employees during the Great Depression was important to residents. In those days many woodworkers were craftsmen of great skill. Though almost everything was done with hand tools, their finished products were of a high quality that is rarely seen today.

In early 1942, Bellevue businessman Phillip Toman purchased the boat works, and changed the name to Kirkland Marine Construction. Toman obtained a contract to build 68 wooden-hulled 38-foot picket boats for the U.S. Coast Guard—the largest Coast Guard contract up to that time. With partner Carl Ballard, Toman built a second structure on the site to house office space, parts storage, and two side-by-side assembly lines for constructing the boats.

The 38-foot picket boats were fast, single-screw harbor patrol craft. Lessons learned with these small fighting boats would later help U.S. riverine forces operating in the humid deltas of Vietnam during the 1960s.

At its peak Kirkland Marine Construction employed about 50 people and had three on-site Coast Guard personnel who made test runs on Lake Washington in the new boats. Unfortunately, like many other local businesses, the firm went under after the war. Apartments now stand on the site of the 'other' shipyard.

Interior of the Kirkland Marine Construction, boat hulls in various stages of completion. Boat were built inverted and then turned to finish with engine and deck. A civilian Inspector is seen talking with work crew. There were always two Coast Guard inspectors and one civilian inspector on hand during work hours to oversee the construction.

A post-World War II view from the air. The large estate with the long driveway, toward the top of the photo, is the Shumway Mansion in its original location.

103

Denton family members seen at the South Kirkland Park at the foot of Seventh Avenue South, the site of today's Brink Park, in 1952. The Ballinger facility is in the background.

Kirkland's southern entrance, near Ballinger, was for years guarded by two World War I field pieces. At the urging of former American Legion Warren O. Grimm Post Commander H. P. "Dick" Everest, the War Department donated a total of four artillery pieces as a war memorial.

1916: "Build the canal, and build it in '93!"

In 1916 crews opened the Montlake Cut, joining Lake Union and Lake Washington and lowering the latter nine feet. The Lake Washington Ship Canal formally opened on July 4, 1917

Water was the highway to the future for the region's settlers. A canal connecting Lake Washington, Lake Union and Puget Sound, they thought, would open vast opportunities for industrializing Lake Washington. Eastside boosters had differing visions for their communities after a canal was built.

South Bellevue was to become a metropolis based on coal mining, Mercer Island wanted the Navy yard (Bremerton eventually got it), and Kirkland was to become The Pittsburgh of the Pacific, a steel exporting center for the world. A canal would also help move the products of Eastside timber harvests. Powerful Seattle-area industrialists formed an association to lobby the government for the canal. Their motto was "Build the canal, and build it in '93!"

There were several efforts to build the canal, beginning in the 1880s. One group went bankrupt after spending $250,000—an incredible sum then—trying to dig a 16-foot wide by 12-foot-deep canal. Work finally got underway in earnest in 1911, with the U.S. Army Corps of Engineers overseeing the digging and lock construction.

Ninety year old former Kirkland baseball player Deep Higginbotham said in 1993 that he remembered watching the excavations as a small boy. He said workers armed with picks and shovels filled wagons with dirt, which mule teams hauled away.

The big day came in July, 1916. Lake Washington rushed through the new canal after crews completed the cut. The lake was nine feet higher then than it is now, and it drained an inch every 24 hours to reach its present level. The lowering left Kirkland docks high and dry and Juanita Bay too shallow for steamer traffic.

The locks connecting Puget Sound to Salmon Bay and Lake Union opened formally on July 4, 1917, but the new canal at Montlake came too late for Peter Kirk and most of the others who had hoped to industrialize the Eastside.

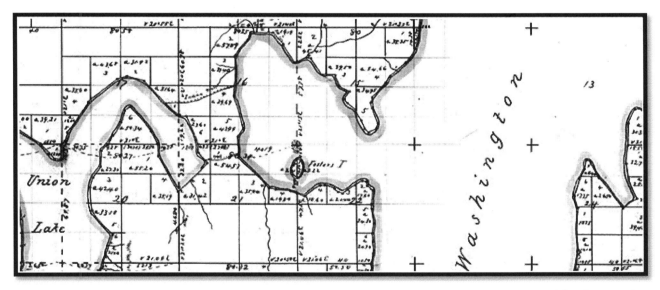

In January 1856 just two trails existed to link Lake Washington and Lake Union. Later a log ditch, and finally a canal, would join the water bodies, and a lower Lake Washington would have a new shoreline.

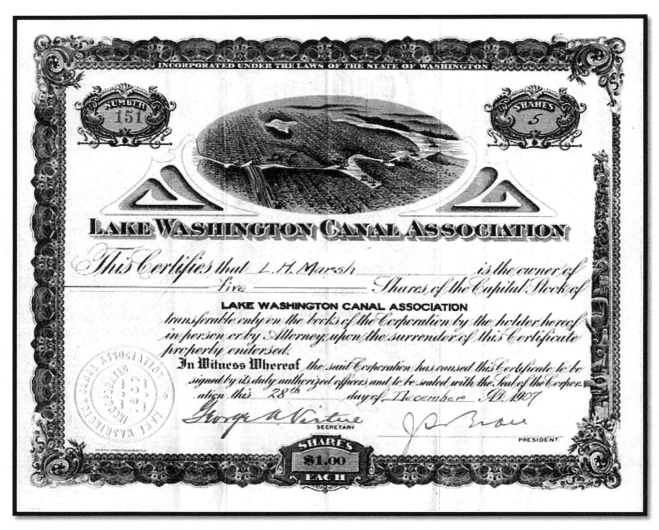

Like many in the area, Ludwig "Lute" Marsh invested in the Lake Washington Canal Association, an organization dedicated to connecting Lake Washington and Lake Union to saltwater. Its president, John Brace, owned J. S. Brace & Company, which operated a substantial sawmill on Lake Union, the Brace & Hergert Lumber Company. Brace died in 1918, living just long enough to see Puget Sound connected by locks to Lake Union, the Montlake Canal, and Lake Washington.

Portage Bay before the Cut—looking north, Portage Bay is in the foreground, with Montlake, Union Bay, and Laurelhurst beyond. Kirkland is visible well beyond Webster Point, in the far distance, along the lake's eastern shore. A narrow ditch was cut to facilitate moving logs out of Lake Washington, below, but it was not navigable by vessels.

Many Kirklanders watched Lake Washington Ship Canal construction with eager anticipation.

The canal connected Lake Washington to salt water, as evidenced by the presence of this seagoing vessel in Lake Washington.

Members of the Mickelson family of Juanita are seen playing on a Juanita beach shortly after the lake was lowered, leaving docks like the one in the background high and dry.

High and dry dock pilings west of Market Street. Note the dry rot at about nine feet above water level on the piling behind the woman on the left. The dry rot at that level is evidence of the pre-Montlake Cut lake level.

In 1917, the Lake Washington Ship Canal officially opened, with much excitement, fanfare, and streams of vessels. Seen here in the Montlake Cut, is the *SS Roosevelt*—the celebrated ship Admiral Robert E. Peary commanded in his 1909 expedition to the North Pole.

Houghton's pioneer Harry French, or perhaps his daughter, Olivia (French) Davis (1896-1945), took this photo of the *SS Roosevelt* the same day as the ship passed in front of the French homestead.

1877: Mr. & Mrs. Forbes Come to Juanita Bay

Eliza and Dorr Forbes came west from Iowa in the 1870s and settled at Juanita Bay.

The story of Juanita's "first family" was first preserved back in the late 1930s. With a pen and the back of an envelope, the late Dorris (Forbes) Beecher sat on a porch with her grandmother, Eliza (Waggener) Forbes (1849-1942), and began recording the historic Forbes saga. Though Eliza was getting old (she had been widowed for nearly two decades) her mind was clear and sharp.

113

Mrs. Beecher's first name was spelled *Dorris* rather than the conventional *Doris,* to honor her late grandfather, Dorr. Eliza and her husband Dorr Forbes (1841-1919) arrived on Seattle's primitive waterfront in 1877 with two young sons and all their belongings. In 1861, at age 20, and in the first year of the Civil War, Dorr enlisted and served as a mounted scout and sharpshooter with E Company of the 33rd Illinois Infantry Regiment of Volunteers—a battle-hardened unit which saw considerable action, including the Siege of Vicksburg. He was wounded in action and discharged in 1863.

After the war, Dorr moved to Iowa where he became a cattle buyer and farmer. There, he met a young teacher, Eliza Ann Waggener. The two married in 1874 and were soon planning their move west. In 1876 the couple and their young son, Ray, boarded an emigrant train in Knoxville, Iowa, and rode the train for two weeks until it finally reached Sacramento, California.

The family then boarded a ship in San Francisco and traveled north to Hillsboro, Oregon where they took up residence in a log cabin. Shortly thereafter a second son, Leon, was born. Eliza and the boys remained at the cabin, but Dorr made a trip north to scout the opportunities in Puget Sound country. He returned with a favorable report and the family took a boat to Kalama, Washington, then a train to Tacoma, where they boarded a Seattle-bound steamer. They stayed overnight in Seattle, then a rough-and-tumble logging town and seaport, at the old New England Hotel.

The next day, the family hauled their possessions by horse drawn wagon over the hill to Lake Washington to a spot derisively called Fleaburg—today's Leschi—a flea-infested Native American settlement with only one permanent cabin. There they loaded everything onto a steamer so tiny Eliza told Dorris years later that it "looked more like a ship's boat."

The steamer chugged north, and Eliza said her apprehension about the move melted when she first laid eyes on Juanita Bay. She said there wasn't a soul in sight, just a beautiful bay surrounded by giant trees. She said she knew at that moment that Juanita was where she wanted to live.

The family's first home site was near the northwest corner of the intersection of what became N.E. 116th Street and 100th Avenue N.E. They had one neighbor, Martin Hubbard. Although at that time the community was called Hubbard, the name Juanita was coming into use. Their first house had already been constructed in Seattle, and they had it hauled to the foot of Madison Street and then barged it across the lake and dragged it up to its final position, which must have been quite a task. During their first year in Juanita they had a third son, Allen. The small community was soon joined (in 1877) by Charles and Mary Dunlap (1850-1908) and their four children. Charles Dunlap (1846-86) was also a Union Army veteran who had fought with I Company of the 4th Iowa Cavalry. Dunlap worked as a school teacher. The Forbes and Dunlap families had known each other in Iowa.

In the early 1880s, Dorr attempted to raise cranberries on additional property they homesteaded on Rose Hill at Forbes Lake. He lost his war with the beavers and sold that property in 1889 to the Kirkland Land & Improvement Company. It later became the site of the Great Western Iron & Steel Works.

Eliza gave birth to their fourth son, Leslie, or "Les" as he was known, in 1886 at their first home. Soon thereafter the couple built a second home off today's 97th Avenue N.E., and Dorr built a shingle mill nearby on Juanita Creek. Hubbard worked there with him, and the two also logged trees from Finn Hill and the surrounding area.

Among their friends were other noted Eastside pioneers, Ole (1837-1914) and Marit Josten (1840-1913), who homesteaded 160 acres at the site of today's Juanita High School; Bothell founders, David (1820-1905) and Mary Anne Bothell (1823-1907); and Woodinville founders Ira (1833-1906) and Susan Woodin (1848-1919). Like Dorr Forbes, both men were Union Army veterans. Mrs. Beecher said her grandmother and fellow pioneer woman Susan Woodin were good friends. Susan Woodin often walked from her homestead in what became Woodinville, to stay overnight at the Forbes home and then the next day cross the lake to Seattle by rowboat or canoe, where she landed at the foot of Madison Street, and then walked the three miles to downtown Seattle to sell butter. Then she walked back to the lake, crossed by small boat, stayed overnight at the Forbes place, and from there walked back home. Susan Woodin, a tough example of a pioneer woman, was also Woodinville's postmistress.

Eliza said during her early years that she was frightened one day when a group of Indians showed up at her door. They were migratory group, however, with peaceful intentions. All they wanted was to warm their feet at the stove inside.

On January 23, 1887 Eliza was the first woman elected justice of the peace on the west coast. In Washington Territory women could vote before it was possible in most of the rest of country. When Washington became a state in 1889, women lost that right and Eliza had to step down from office. She remained a political activist and had a large photograph of Teddy Roosevelt prominently displayed in her living room. She frequently attended Republican Party meetings in Seattle. Mrs. Beecher recalled that once when Eliza was in her late 80s she made the trip across the lake to one party function and fell and broke her arm. Undaunted, she returned home and her daughter-in-law, Alicia Forbes, got Dr. George Davis to splint the broken arm. But Eliza stubbornly refused to wear the splint. Despite her uncooperation, her arm healed perfectly.

In her later years, a Forbes family member typically provided transportation for Eliza, but if a family member was not available, she didn't let that stop her. She'd call the jitney (taxi) in Kirkland to come pick her up and take her to the ferry so she could attend Republican Party meetings. When she was in her 90s, her sons asked the jitney operators to refuse to fetch her when she called. This did not stop her. One time she disappeared, causing her family to launch a search. They heard from a neighbor that he'd seen her out on the road hitching a ride to the ferry. Eliza Forbes did what Eliza Forbes wanted to do.

Another time, again in her later years, Eliza disappeared for the day, but returned very excited. As a young woman in the 1800s she'd had a dream one night that she was flying in a machine that carried passengers through the sky. This dream was years prior to the first powered flight. Eliza disappearance turned out to be a visit to Seattle where she flew in an airplane to Bremerton and back. She claimed the experience was her dream coming true. At the time of her adventure, few Kirkland-area residents and certainly no other member of the Forbes family had flow in an airplane. This feisty pioneer grandma was the first.

King County owned the 1905 Forbes house from 1956 until 2002, when the City of Kirkland acquired Juanita Beach Park. The family extensively remodeled it in 1937, so its appearance has changed since 1905, but it still stands on its original site at 11829 97th Ave. N.E. Mrs. Beecher said her grandparents planted the fruit trees around the home, which still produce fruit.

Mrs. Beecher said that even into her pioneer grandmother's senior years she caught fish in Juanita Creek, then a thriving salmon stream as well as home to trout and other edible species. She also picked stinging nettles, dandelions, and wild berries, all of which were a regular part of their diets. Mrs. Beecher said Eliza also enjoyed sitting on porch and shooting robins from her fruit trees with a .22 rifle. Pioneers considered robin's breast a culinary delicacy. She lived the life of a rugged, individualistic pioneer, right up to her death in 1942.

This is what Eliza and Dorr Forbes saw from the old New England Hotel on their first day in Seattle in 1877. This 1875 photo taken looks up First Avenue from South Main Street. Seattle was then a rough-and-tumble western lumber town and seaport. The hill was called Denny's Knoll and has been softened somewhat through regrading since that time. The highest building, with the cupola, was the old Territorial University, the earliest incarnation of the University of Washington, which did not move to its present Portage Bay location until 1895. The Territorial University also offered primary school classes. Though the structure dates to 1861, it was not until 1876 that it had its first graduate, Clara McCarty. She went on to a teaching career and in 1879 was elected Pierce County's superintendent of schools. (Information compiled from several HistoryLink.org essays, a veritable treasure trove of additional information on early Seattle and Washington history—a highly recommended source.)

Dorr and Eliza built their house, seen as 1880s. It was their second house at Juanita, off 97th Avenue N.E. When it burned in 1905, the couple built a new home on the same property.

In addition to his shingle mill, Dorr Forbes was a logger. He had a contract to cut cordwood, which was used to fuel the early Lake Washington steamboats.

View looking south at Lake Washington in 1913, down today's 97th Avenue N.E., then called Bothell Road. The Forbes home was on the right, at their mailbox.

Susan Woodin, Woodinville co-founder, was a tough, independent pioneer woman, and a close friend of Eliza Forbes.

The marker on the Forbes' graves.

An early view of the Lake House and members of the Fish family—in the front are John, Abigail, and daughter Bessie.

If you lived in Redmond, Duvall, or Fall City in the 1880s, the trip to Seattle for supplies took at least two days. The old Curtis Road to Redmond—it became N.E. 52nd Street—met the lakeshore at Houghton, and from there travelers caught a steamer to Madison Park.

All this made Houghton a logical overnight stop at the Lake House, which was Houghton's finest hotel. In fact, it was also the only hotel. The Lake House, one of the first frame structures in the area, was built as Captain Jay C. and Eve O'Conner's private home in the early 1880s. It was then located on the lakeshore, on the east side of today's Lake Washington Boulevard, across from Houghton Beach.

Captain O'Conner is remembered for his steamboat activities. As travelers increased in numbers business at the hotel increased. Eve O'Conner ran the hotel in addition to the normal chores pioneer women performed. In 1884, after several years of operating both of their businesses, the O'Conners sold the Lake

House.

The Fishes came west from Maine. There were ten in all: the two parents, five sons, and three daughters. When they arrived in Houghton, they bought the Lake House and its accompanying ten acres from the O'Conners for $3,000. The decision proved a wise move. Less than two months after they bought the land they sold two of the acres for more than they had paid for the entire parcel.

The father, John Fish, was nearly blind, so much of the work fell on his wife, Abigail, and their children. A typical work day for Abigail began at 5 a.m. and continued straight through until 9 p.m. In those days washing clothes took many hours, as did baking, feeding cows and chickens, and making—by hand—many of the products we take for granted today, such as soap.

Like most settlers, the Fishes raised much of their own food in their gardens, in addition to their livestock. Abigail also fed hotel guests, and she had a reputation as one of the best cooks around.

Eventually, the Lake House was passed on to the Fishes' daughter, Ida Elizabeth "Bessie" (1872-1958), and her husband, Erastus Kirtley (1852-1923). They operated the business as a hotel and Erastus, who was said to dislike his first name and always corresponded as E. Kirtley, added a stage line which ran to North Bend. E. Kirtly was himself of pioneer stock—he was a one year-old baby when his family brought him to the Washington Territory in 1854 and worked as a logger prior to marrying Bessie. Bessie and Erastus passed the Lake House on to their son Frank (1895-1989) and his wife Beatrice (1897-1982). At about the start of World War II the Lake House ceased hotel operations.

The Lake House was eventually sold. It was razed in 1984. The site is now occupied by an office building. Historical markers stand where the Lake House's once stood, a spot from which the Fishes and many of Houghton's other residents watched the smoke and glow of the great Seattle fire in 1889.

The Lake House passed to Ida Elizabeth "Bessie" (Fish) Kirtley and her husband Erastus Kirtley. The couple's descendants operated the business until World War II.

The Lake House, as seen just before its 1984 demolition. It was located at 10127 N.E. 59th Street.

Abigail Fish was so fascinated by having seen the glow of the Great Seattle fire of 1889 that she purchased cabinet photos, including this one, of the fire's aftermath.

PRINCESS ANGELINE

Princess Angeline was of the Duwamish People. She was Chief Sealth's (Chief Seattle) daughter. Angeline was a popular late 19th century Seattle celebrity who supplemented her living by selling images of herself. Bessie Fish purchased this one from Angeline in the 1890s.

Early steamboat captain Ed Niblock (1879-1928) and his horse Recall.

It has been a long time since livestock could be seen grazing at the intersection of Central Way and Market Street. But if you look closely at the photo above you can see cattle on the hillside; they're on the left, behind steamboat captain Ed Niblock and his horse Recall.

Old-time Kirklanders remember the old bank building, which housed the Lake Washington Telephone Company and a variety of other ventures over the years. The bank building was Kirkland's first brick structure, erected in 1888 by Peter Kirk and his partners.

The building originally served as the steel mill's offices. Kirk also used the building for his Kirkland Land and Improvement Company, which remained under Kirk's control until the development firm Burke and Farrar purchased the business in 1910. Never willing to give up on his dream of seeing Kirkland developed, Kirk promptly reinvested some of the sales proceeds back into Burke and Farrar's land development business.

In 1911, Glenn Johnson founded the Kirkland State Bank on the first floor of the building, which was how it became known as the bank building.

Telephone service in Kirkland began under a franchise granted in 1907 to T. L. Kyler and James Bell (Peter Kirk's son-in-law). It stipulated that they had to provide free service to several prominent citizens' homes.

David Burr came to Kirkland in 1914 and bought 40 percent of the phone company in 1915. Burr said in a 1948 newspaper interview that the system then had 250 customers and that some became indignant when they discovered he expected them to pay their phone bills. One finally paid up when Burr climbed the pole in front of the man's home, and began disconnecting his phone.

The four phone exchanges were Red, Black, Main, and Farmers. Main 6 got you the Brooks Grocery and Red 421 rang at L.L. Forbes' Juanita Beach. Some were on party lines that served as many as 20 customers per line. The business was the first independent phone company in Washington to install an automatic dial exchange, and it eventually moved to a newer building on Central Way. When Burr sold the business in 1943 there were 1,800 subscribers. It later became the West Coast Telephone and then GTE.

The bank building was razed in the 1950s and the site became a parking lot for the GTE Building. (**2010 Update**: In 1998 the old Bank Building site was developed into the Tiara de Lago condo and retail project. The GTE Building is now called the Frontier Building).

Bank Building

This view from the lake (c. 1890) shows the Bank Building. At this time crews from the Kirkland Land and Improvement Company were clearing the town site. Much of the underbrush and trees were burned away, and the smoke from these fires is visible in this photo. Some Kirklanders who witnessed this as children later lamented the wasted timber value of these first growth trees, though many of these giants growing nearer the mill site at Forbes Lake were cut into lumber at the enterprise sawmill, which was located on the steel mill compound.

The Kirkland State Bank opened in 1911, at 210 Market Street.

This view of the same building, in 1930.

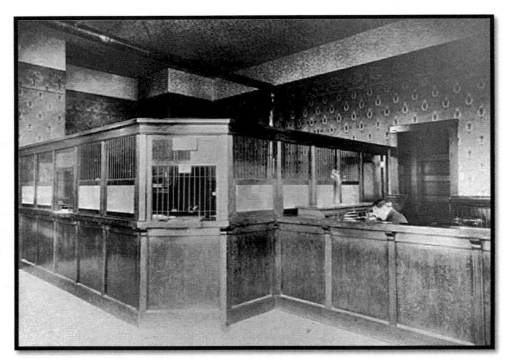

The first floor interior of the bank.

This pre-1916 view faces northwest across Moss Bay and shows the Bank Building before the lake was lowered.

A rare 1933 photo of the Bank Building's upstairs interior, the offices of David Burr, the owner of the Lake Washington Telephone Company.

David Burr atop a Kirkland fire pump truck on Lake Street, about 1920. Standing are Joe Scavella, Jim Reese, Ed Williams, and Ed Blau. Visible in the background is Klenert's Meat Market and Burke & Farrar's real estate office.

David Burr, Jr climbs the telephone pole in front of the Bank Building in 1924.

This small structure was attached to the east side of the Bank Building. The barely-readable slogan on the siding reads: "Kirkland, the Oakland of Seattle." Radio and film star Lancelot "Lanny" Ross was born in that little building on January 19, 1906.

Lanny Ross in a 1950 *Look Magazine* cigarette advertisement.

Lanny Ross performing in a 1930s radio broadcast.

130

1901: The "Miserable old King County of Kent"

Kirkland Ferry Dock. Old King Co. Ferry.

The photo was taken about 1901, from the Standard Mill dock which extended into Moss Bay from the end of Market Street. The *King County of Kent* is moored where the Marina Park boat dock stands today.

It was the turn of the century when some Kirklanders convinced the county to build a Lake Washington ferry boat and slips at Kirkland and Madison Park. Evidently, many thought a ferry would give Kirkland's dismal economy a shot in the arm. King County ferry advocates apparently weren't too worried about the government subsidized competition hurting their friends to the south, in Houghton, who depended on private steamboating for their livings.

The county built its ferry dock at the foot of what became Kirkland Avenue. It also contracted a Seattle shipbuilder to construct a steam side-wheel ferry, with a then-revolutionary double end design. The vessel, the *King County of Kent*, was built at Madison Park by the Moran Brothers, although they had no shipyard there.

The *King County of Kent* began earning her reputation as a jinxed boat on the day she was launched. Loaded with political and civic dignitaries, she slid down the ways into the lake, where she promptly grounded just off shore on a mud bank, leaving her party stranded for several hours while crews muscled her free.

Although Kirkland's ferry dock did usher in a few small businesses, the county's involvement in lake transportation proved costly to taxpayers and undercut private operators. The county losses from its ferry fleet eventually reached $100,000, a considerable sum at that time.

Private steam boaters had to adapt or perish. One popular trick to outsmart the county was to pull one's private steamer into the county dock just before the county boat was scheduled to arrive, to pick up passengers, and quickly get out of the way.

The county sued Captain John Anderson for $10,000 for doing that one too many times. Both sides initiated numerous lawsuits over the years.

The *King County of Kent* was plagued by problems. She was poorly constructed, her machinery often broke down and oh, yes, she leaked. She ended her brief career in 1908 when she was condemned. Residents wrote about most of the other lake boats during that era using glowing, nostalgic language. Not so for the *King County of Kent*. "Miserable old" *King County of Kent* seems the most common appellation.

The *King County of Kent* became stuck in the mud at her launching in 1900. Things went downhill from that point for the vessel.

1922: Going down to Jackson, Fort Jackson, that is...

Fort Jackson served as Kirkland's American Legion post from 1922 until 1929. It was a fixture on the Kirkland waterfront, tied up just south of the ferry dock. The American Legion post was formed in 1919 by Kirkland's recently-returned World War I veterans.

When World War I came it generated new jobs for residents, but many young Kirkland men went abroad to fight in the mud and trenches of European battlefields. Some never came home. Returning veterans brought the American Legion to Kirkland, in the form of the Warren O. Grimm Post No. 83, on December 12, 1919. The post's first commander was Dr. E.C. McKibben, Sr., who was one of Kirkland's well-liked and much-respected citizens. A.C. "Coal" Newell served as the post's first adjutant. Harold "Dick" Everest was a co-founder.

The Legion has only one aim, the promotion of Patriotism, Americanism, and the whole-hearted support of the constituted authority, its one desire to make our country a better place to live in, wrote Newell in 1922.

The post's founders originally tried to encompass the entire Eastside, rotating meeting locations between Kirkland, Redmond and Bellevue, since there were charter members living in all three towns. The members soon chose Kirkland as the post's permanent location, since they found maintaining three halls difficult.

After the war, nearly 50 war surplus Ferris type wooden freighters crowded Lake Union in a line dubbed Wilson's Wood Row, a sarcastic, derisive reference to President Woodrow Wilson. While most of these vessels ended up in a funeral pyre or crushed beneath the wrecker's hammer, Harold "Dick" Everest of the Warren O. Grimm Post managed to wrangle one of the ships from the United States Fleet Corporation for $3,500.

The post moved the hull to the foot of Second Avenue South, in Kirkland. Named *Fort Jackson*, it became the only floating clubhouse of its type in the world, according to Newell.

Although cash was tight in those days, the post managed to recoup its $3,500 by selling unneeded equipment from the vessel for salvage. Anticipating this, Everest had intentionally selected the *Fort Jackson* because it still contained more equipment than the other available vessels in storage. Soon, the members had converted the ship, adding a dance hall, clubrooms, gym, and other accommodations. Once completed, they made the *Fort Jackson* available for the use of the Boy Scouts, Camp Fire Girls, and other community organizations.

The Legion and its associated Women's Auxiliary—composed of wives, sisters, and mothers of ex-service men—used the vessel until 1929, when the group acquired the former Kirkland Baptist Church Building on Fifth Avenue, which still stands across from today's city hall.

The *Fort Jackson*, which had settled into the muddy lake bottom, developed dry rot and other costly maintenance issues so the post sold her for scrap, and after two tugboats struggled all morning to wrest her from the muck, she was towed into Puget Sound where she was scrapped and then burned at Richmond Beach.

Interestingly, some of the post's founding members' sons were themselves eligible for Legion membership when they returned to Kirkland from serving in World War II.

Warren O. Grimm American Legion Post members dedicate the old Kirkland Gateway in 1923.

LEGION POST KIRKLAND WASH.

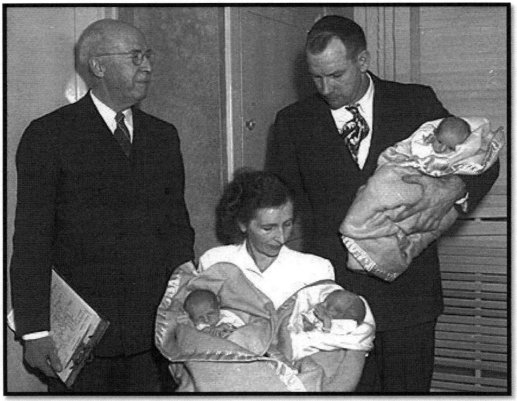

Dr. E.C. McKibben, Sr., left, was a post co-founder. He is shown here after delivering the Eastside's first triplets.

Warren O. Grimm Post co-founder H.P. "Dick" Everest (1894-1967), as a US Army lieutenant during World War I. Everest's family came to Kirkland in 1888 during the Kirk era boom, and he was very prominent in Kirkland business and civic life. He edited the *Eastside Journal* newspaper during the 1920-30s, and Everest Park is named for him. Everest graduated from high school in 1912 and earned bachelor's and master's degrees in science at the University of Washington and became President of the Kirkland Investment Company and publisher of the *East Side Journal* newspaper for 16 years. He became a professor in the University of Washington School of Communications and became the school's president in 1944. He was appointed acting President of the University of Washington in 1951-1952 and went on to serve as Vice President until retiring in 1957.

Interior view of the *Fort Jackson.*

The *Fort Jackson* being moved from Lake Union to Kirkland.

The *Fort Jackson* nameplate was spared, and is on display at the Kirkland Heritage Society Resource Center.

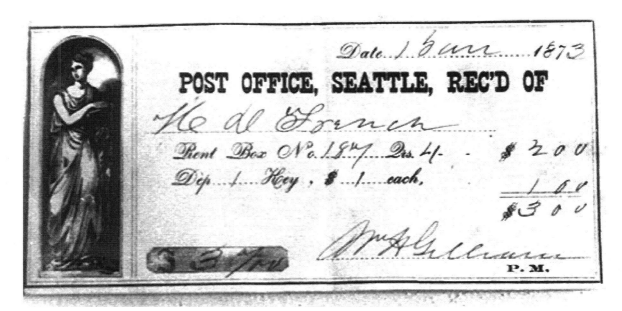

Receiving letters was important to Houghton pioneer Harry French. He rented a post office box so he would be sure to get his mail. This is a receipt for his first box. In 1873 the box rental was $3 for one year.

Houghton pioneer Harry French's (1849-1937) journals reveal a man of strong character. And character mattered when it came to carving a settlement out of the giant trees and thick sticker bushes lining Lake Washington's eastern shore.

French kept journals that provide interesting insights into his daily life and activities. Kirkland Heritage Society has most of these journals (from the 1870s), the decade he came west from Maine. Harry arrived in Seattle with his parents, Samuel and Caroline, on July 2, 1872, when he was 22 years old. He stayed only a few days before traveling to the White River area, near Auburn, to work on a farm.

There he met Thomas Popham, who lived in an area south of Kirkland that was known to settlers as "Lake Washington," and would later become known as Houghton. Thomas lived there with his mother and brother. At the time they were the sole settlers south of Juanita Bay. Samuel and Caroline considered buying the Popham's land, but decided instead to buy the claim of Alfred Smith, which was just north of the Popham property. They consummated their purchase on August 3. A month later, Harry gave Jay C. O'Conner $22 for the right to his claim, adjacent to Samuel's.

Today's N.E. 63rd Street divided their two 80-acre tracts. Harry worked hard clearing land until November, when he rented a house in Seattle for the winter months.

In 1872, there was plenty of trouble available for an interested young man in Seattle.

Among white people, the ratio of men to women was over 20 to 1. It was a wild frontier town. Drinking and gambling were popular diversions, and brothels—staffed largely by American Indian women and called squaw houses—were plentiful along the tide flats.

One of these establishments, The Illahee (an Indian word meaning home away from home), provided much of Seattle's tax revenue.

Harry didn't indulge in those activities. He worked hard, first for the Seattle Coal Company, and later at Henry Yesler's sawmill. His social life revolved around church attendance—twice on some Sundays—and he frequented the meetings of other religious and temperance groups.

Harry stayed in Seattle all winter, returning to Houghton in April, 1873. Harry, his father, and his friend Tom Popham, had to take a sizable load of summer supplies to their claims, so the men loaded their gear onto a coal train near the waterfront. They paid 50 cents to have their freight transported to the coal company depot on Lake Union, where it was shipped, for another 50 cents, by barge to the portage between Portage Bay and what became the Montlake Cut. It is possible they used Sam French's Indian canoe to transport their supplies across the lake to their claims. The transportation took them two days.

When the French family began their first full summer at Houghton they had been in the region for nearly a year. Harry's journals reveal his pecuniary character. He accounted for every dime he earned and he didn't appear to waste a cent.

By the end of 1873, young Harry owned 80 acres of land on Lake Washington and had saved $35—a healthy sum for that time.

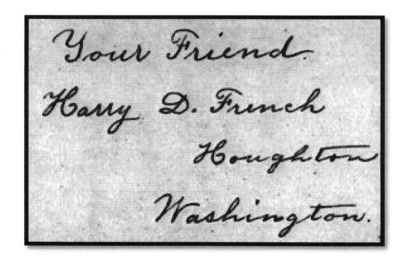

Harry D. French in the 1880s.

French later in life (in the 1930s).

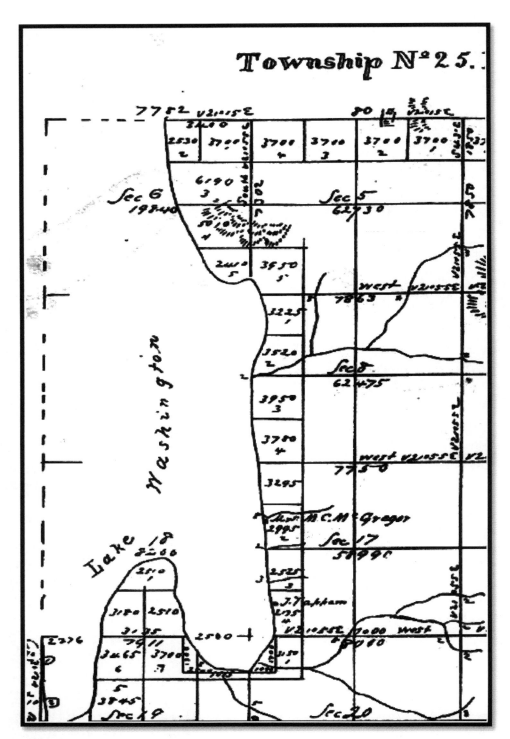

The 1870 survey map (above) shows the claims of James Popham—misidentified as "Tahham" by the surveyors-- and Mrs. Nancy McGregor, his mother. In the short time the Pophams lived on Lake Washington the brothers shot six cougars. Bear steak was a popular, inexpensive protein source.

1874: Harry D. French and his Life on Lake Washington

In front of his frame house, Harry French, left, stands beside his mother, Caroline, and his father, Sam. With them are John Tuttle and Lucy (Tuttle) Stamp. The French House was moved from its original site, but still stands in Houghton. It is the oldest frame dwelling on the Eastside.

Harry French began 1874 working for Henry Yesler at Yesler's Seattle sawmill. His father, Sam French, had been sick with painter's colic. He was treated by Seattle's Dr. Bagley and he recovered. When the French family moved back to their Lake Washington (Houghton) claims they had more neighbors than in the previous summer. Harry got to work clearing his land.

In those days large old-growth trees covered the area. Removing them was the top priority. A popular technique of the day was "boring." French drilled a hole in the tree's trunk and set a small fire inside. The tree burned until it toppled. A settler could bore many more trees in a day than he could fell with an ax.

Considering today's wood prices, it might seem strange that, once on the ground, most of the trees were simply piled up and burned—a practice that continued into this century, as some Kirkland seniors can attest. Harry uses some of the felled timber to make his split rail fence and for construction. Clearing a pasture of forest was an incredible amount of work in a time before bulldozers and chain saws. It was probably the reason he wanted a photograph of the results of his labor (below).

Harry had a crude cabin, but he began building Kirkland's first house that year. He and his friend Tom Popham spent a day paddling an Indian canoe all the way up the Sammamish River to Ira Woodin's place (Woodinville) to borrow Woodin's scow. Woodin wasn't home, so they came back the next day. This time they just paddled up to "Wannita Bay" (Juanita Bay) and hiked the trail through the forest that led to the Woodin's cabin. There they found Woodin, who agreed to loan his scow. They carried it all the way back down the trail to Juanita Bay.

They needed Woodin's scow to transport the lumber and bricks across the lake for Harry's house. It took several days to haul the materials from McGilvira's Landing, as Madison Park was known then. The men seemed to have loaded the scow to the gunnels, for Harry wrote in his journal that he swamped the boat several times.

An early view of the French House and split rail fence, looking north.

Caroline French (1827-1909), Harry French's mother and a Lake Washington pioneer.

Caroline French, seen in 1908 with her granddaughter Olivia (French) Davis (1896-1945). Olivia was the daughter of Harry and Rosa (Jones) French (1857-1956). Harry and Rosa were married in 1895. Olivia married Cuba Davis (1894-1977) in 1921.

1994: The Kirkland Oral History Project

Former *East Side Journal* owner Charles "Chuck" Morgan (1911-2009), left, and former Kirkland mayor and 48th District legislator Al Leland (1921-1995). Both men volunteered as Kirkland History Project narrators. Leland was Kirkland's youngest mayor, elected at 29, and while in the Washington State Legislature his staunch advocacy of freeway building earned him the nickname "Concrete Al."

Without residents' help, Community histories are often dry repositories of information recorded in little-read volumes or academic works. People breathe life into these facts with their memories, photographs, and memorabilia.

Long-time residents made Kirkland's history the interesting story that it should be. In recent years Kirklanders have demonstrated their concern for their community's past. On March 12, 1994 the Kirkland History Project narrators and interviewers gathered at the Kirkland Library. The city-sponsored project was a year-long project to gather oral histories and index the old *East Side Journal* newspaper. More than 100 people were nominated as oral history narrators, but unfortunately volunteer interviewers couldn't get to everyone so interviews will continue under the auspices of the Kirkland Heritage Society.

Some attending the meetings who have already been interviewed include recently retired Kirkland City Councilwoman Doris Cooper, former Mayor Al Leland, former City Manager

Allen Locke, former *East Side Journal* Publisher Charles Morgan, photographer Ernie Fortesque, and many others. One interesting, not yet interviewed attendee was Mabel (Andreen) Stuesdall. She proudly told the group that she was born in Kirkland in 1896 and even brought her 1914 Kirkland High School diploma.

Kirkland's Assistant City Manager, Andy Barton presented the volunteers with certificates of appreciation, and volunteers Joan McBride and Alan Stein also addressed group. Project Director Lorraine McConaghy, said she hopes to learn more about Cort's Whisker Retreat, frequented by Seattle's rather bohemian theatre people, known for its wildness and its guests' colorful activities.

Of course, Kirkland Heritage Society is always looking for pre-*East Side Journal* Kirkland newspapers, old home movies, and photographs (to copy before returning to the owners). Project narrators kindly loaned materials for duplication. Sharing these materials makes an important contribution. Most "Look to the Past" photographs are copies of originals that once sat in people's basements and attics. With local history, a person need not have been either rich or famous to be important—they just needed to have been there. The stories about regular, everyday folks are the most interesting.

If you have any old photographs, movies, or pre-1919 Kirkland newspapers that you would like to share for duplication—we never ask to keep lenders' originals—you can reach me, Matt McCauley, at (425) 827-3446, at the Kirkland Heritage Society.

Dr. Ernest C. "Ernie" McKibben, Jr. was born in Kirkland in 1920 and, like his father, former Kirkland mayor, Dr. Ernest C. McKibben, Sr., served in the US Army and went on to practice medicine in Kirkland. Both men rate among Kirkland's most beloved and well-respected citizens. Dr. McKibben, Jr. volunteered as a narrator in the 1994 Kirkland History Project and has a longstanding commitment to recording and documenting Kirkland's past.

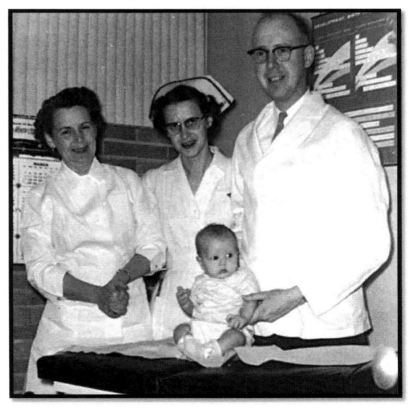

Dorris (Forbes) Beecher, center, poses at Juanita Beach in 1922 with her cousins Selma and Bernice. The author interviewed Mrs. Beecher, a Kirkland History Project volunteer narrator, in 1994. She provided invaluable memories and photos of her family, who first came to Juanita in 1877. The structures in the background are Harry Langdon's Juanita Grocery and his commercial garage, located at the intersection of today's N.E. 116th Street and 100th Avenue N.E., then called "Juanita Junction."

A view of Eyanson's woolen mill. The mill was built in 1892 and for a time was Kirkland's only industry, employing between 150 to 250 people. Though located in Kirkland, it was named "Seattle Woolen Company," which has led to some confusion.

In 1890, when Kirkland enjoyed a period of economic boom period, Englishman Peter Kirk and his business partners tried to attract other industries to Kirkland. Because they were in the land development business in addition to being in the steel manufacturing business, they sought to create more demand for property in the town site they owned.

Kirk's colorful American partner, Leigh Hunt, enticed Edward Eyanson (1864-1932), of Columbia City, Indiana, to relocate his wool processing operation to Kirkland. Although Hunt was a promoter's promoter, Eyanson's decision to move here nevertheless made good business sense. First, because his would be the only woolen mill in Washington, and second because wool processing required clean, pure water and Lake Washington's water quality would allow him to manufacture wool two grades coarser than was available in other parts of the country.

Eyanson erected his facility on the lake near the foot of Fourth Street West and began operation in 1892. Ironically, although the Kirk partners had recruited Eyanson's venture as a side-show industry, it was Eyanson who remained in business after most of the Kirk partners went bust in the 1893 financial panic. After the crash the Eyanson's Seattle Woolen Company was Kirkland's only industry.

The mill's first superintendent was James Barrie, a skilled woolen tradesman, who came to Kirkland in 1895 with his wife Margaret and grown son Robert and his wife Lucy (Griswold)

Barrie. Robert worked for a time at the mill, but was a carpenter by trade who helped build some of Boeing's first wood and fabric biplanes. He also umpired many local baseball games. His wife, Lucy, was the daughter of Redmond pioneer Isaac Griswold, a Civil War cavalry officer. She is well remembered for operating a lunch counter on Waverly Way, across from the old Union "A" High School

Production at Eyanson's Mill increased in the late 1890s during the 1896 Klondike Gold Rush. In that year Eyanson expanded by opening a retail store in Seattle, which sold mackinaws and other woolen goods to Alaska-bound prospectors.

Senior Kirklanders, who—braving parental scoldings—swam near the mill as small children in the 1910s, say they remember having to avoid the slicks of foaming, dirty water that the mill occasionally discharged straight into the lake. One remembered that on the days the mill dyed wool, the water near the mill was colored by that dye. He said yellow dye made the lake look the strangest.

The Seattle Woolen Mill was Kirkland's primary employer in the last half of the 1890s.

The steamer *Kirkland* heads toward her namesake town in the early 1890s. The road going up the hill on the left is Market Street and the smoke at the left is coming from Eyanson's woolen mill.

The mill staff in 1900.

Robert Barrie (1868-1931) came to Kirkland in 1895 with his parents. He and his father, James, worked in Edward Eyanson's woolen mill at its startup. James set up the machinery and Robert was a foreman. He also worked with his friend, noted photographer of Native Americans, Edward Curtis. He finished his career at the Boeing Airplane Company. Seen here with his wife, Lucy (Griswold) Barrie (1876-1970). She is fondly remembered by today's senior Kirklanders because she ran a small lunch counter business from her home at 100 Waverly Way, across the street from Kirkland's Union "A" High School and Kirkland Junior High School from 1932 to 1951.

Renowned Pacific Northwest photographer Asahel Curtis witnessed the Barrie's marriage in 1894. Barrie worked with Asahel's older brother, Edward Curtis, and was a friend to both.

Members of the Barrie family walking along the planked sidewalks of Market Street, during the 1910s. The view faces north. Kirk era brick buildings are in the background.

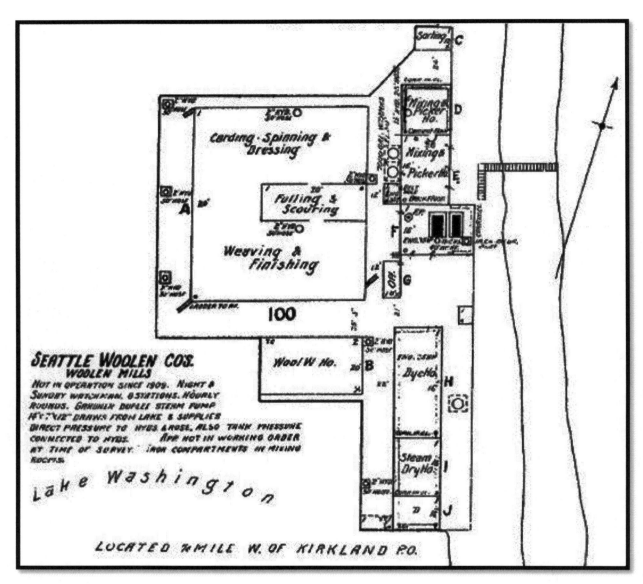

The Seattle Woolen Mill, as described on the 1892 Sanborn Fire Map.

The then-new Matzen Woolen Mill in the 1920s. Once the most efficient woolen mill on the West Coast, its machinery was eventually moved. The building burned to the ground under mysterious circumstances.

Kirklanders watched closely when George Matzen, neither a speculator nor a stranger to manufacturing woolen goods, bought Edward Eyanson's woolen mill in 1915. Matzen began in Seattle in 1902 when he started his business at 14th Avenue and Madison Street, with three employees and $35 in capital. His operation grew, and when the old Eyanson Mill became available, Matzen snatched it up and moved his business to Kirkland.

Renamed the Matzen Woolen Mill, the facility continued to employ Kirklanders, but its output and payroll dramatically increased shortly after the purchase, when World War I created an enormous market for woolen goods. This was a prosperous time for the mill, because demand for its products always exceeded its capacity.

In 1923, a large order jumped the payroll from $100,000 to $150,000, and Matzen reinvested much of his profits into new machinery and expanded facilities. Unfortunately, the entire mill burned to the ground in a fire one year later. Undaunted, Matzen rebuilt the mill as a larger, modern facility. It was one of the finest of its type on the West Coast. At that time the mill's superintendent was Morris Marks, who lived in Juanita—off today's N.E. 132nd Street, where Lakeside-Milem Recovery Center now stands—on a five acre estate called Brookwood. Well-known for its impressive collection of trees and shrubs, tourists came to town just to see Brookwood's gardens.

Before his recent death, O. L. "Deep" Higginbotham, who worked at the mill beginning in 1919, said financial difficulties forced the mill to close for three years, beginning in 1926. He went back to work there after it reopened in 1929 as the National Woolen Mill, under a new owner, Yakima businessman Reese Brown.

Higginbotham said workers were happy to have their jobs back, but working for Brown was not pleasant. He said Brown opened a company store near the corner of Central Way and Lake Street South, where workers, paid in company script, had to trade their script for goods that sold at inflated prices. He said Brown operated the mill for only a short time before it closed once again. Shortly after that Brown was killed in a gruesome traffic accident near Wapato, Washington.

In March 1935, the mill was auctioned off, but the new owners simply stripped most of its machinery for their own mill in Oregon, dashing the dreams of Eastsiders, who had hoped it would reopen and provide jobs as relief from the Great Depression.

A view of the mill from the end of its dock.

Interior view: The machinery was state-of-the-art.

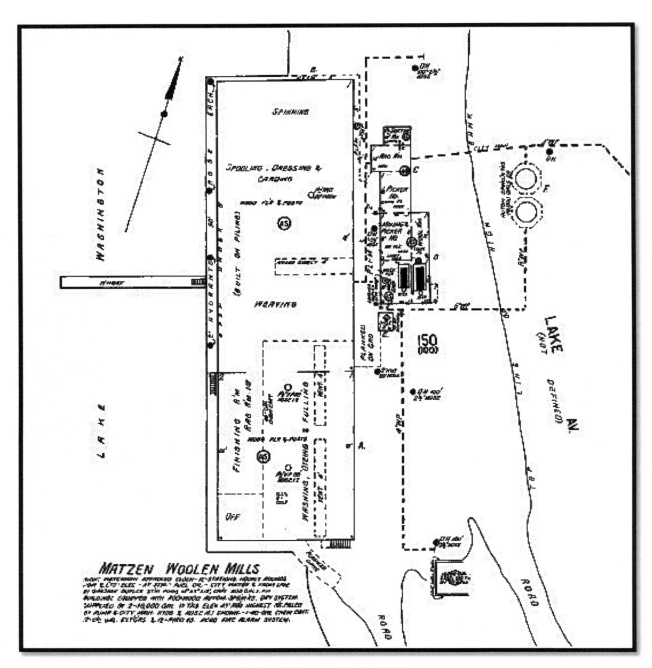

A plan of Matzen Woolen Mills.

This is what street repairs on Lake Street South and Kirkland Avenue looked like in the early 1900s. The crew is planking the road as part of an ambitious improvement project designed to stimulate development. The man controlling the team of horses is Al Tillman.

In honor of the current downtown street repairs, we get this view, taken near the corner of Kirkland Avenue and Lake Street South, probably before 1910. The man driving the team is Al Tillman. Tillman, a World War I veteran, later operated Kirkland Moving and Transfer Company. His wife, Florence (Brooks) Tillman, was the daughter of Emery and Annabelle (Patty) Brooks, who came to Kirkland in about 1890 and were, for many years, the only grocers operating in the city. The Brooks Building, on Market Street, is named after them. They built it in 1905 and operated the business as Pioneer Grocery.

The crew in the photo are laying planks on Kirkland Avenue, at the end of which was the ferry dock. After Kirkland was incorporated in 1905, it was still suffering from an economic slump caused by Kirk's mill failure. In an effort to attract development, the town undertook an ambitious facelift that included street improvement projects such as grading, building sidewalks, and pulling stumps out of the streets. It was all quite a project for a town with a population of 532 (1910 U.S. Census).

According to Arline Ely's *Our Foundering Fathers*, the new taxes to pay for all of the renovations upset some residents, who tried to have the town unincorporated. Voters defeated this effort and the town council went on to enact controversial ordinances, such as limiting to daytime the hours livestock were allowed to roam freely through the downtown area. Well before the rest of the country, Kirkland became a dry town, wherein the selling of liquor was prohibited.

Years later, in 1933, when Prohibition ended nationally, the town council voted three to one to allow beer. The dissenting vote belonged to the mayor, Reverend Charles Newberry, pastor of the Congregational Church. Rev. Newberry said, as a matter of principal, that he could not morally justify preaching against liquor on Sundays and then administer revenues from its sale during the rest of the week.

The Brooks family operated the Pioneer Grocery at four locations beginning in 1890, near the steel mill, on Rose Hill, in the Campbell Building on Market Street, and then in the Hotel Jackson, on the other side of Market Street. The family built their own structure in 1905. It still stands today on Market Street as the Brooks Building. The brick structure on the right was the Jackson Hotel, which also served at Kirkland's first movie theatre during the silent movie era. Later, Kirkland Mayor Al Leland's family operated a car dealership there. It was demolished in the 1960s and local boys were paid to knock the mortar off the old bricks for reuse—they got a nickel per brick. The Jackson Hotel site is now the Leland Place Condominiums.

This 1900s Brooks family photo, taken from their store looking to the northeast, provides an early glimpse of Market Street as a dirt road bordered by a wood sidewalk. The Peter Kirk and Cambell buildings are across the street.

TOWN OF KIRKLAND
COUNTY OF KING
WASHINGTON

To _Peter Kirk_

You are hereby notified that in the assessment roll of Local Improvement District No. _6_
of said Town, the following tracts were assessed for the following amounts in your name:

DESCRIPTION	BLOCK	LOT	AMOUNT
Plat of the Town of Kirkland	36	6	15.26
		7	15.26
		Total	$30.52

Allie W. Patty
Treasurer of the Town of Kirkland, Washington.

By 1905, when Kirkland was incorporated, Peter Kirk had moved to San Juan Island. Nonetheless, he owned real estate in Kirkland until his death in 1916.

Kirkland mayor, Rev. Charles Newberry, seen in 1932 at the lake after swimming in the woolen swimsuits in use at that time. In April, 1933, Newberry resigned as mayor when the Town Council voted to allow alcohol sales, 3.2% beer, in Kirkland. Rev. Newberry said, simply, "Gentlemen, this is my final word on this issue," put his letter of resignation on the table and left the building.

Juanita settler Dorr Forbes built the first bridge linking Kirkland and Juanita in 1890. Forbes and others believed Juanita would be an important shipping center once Kirkland became a thriving steel town. This view faces north. The man on the right side of the photo is unidentified.

In 1890, Kirkland bore little resemblance to the sleepy collection of settler cabins it had been just two years earlier. Peter Kirk's steel mill plans brought speculation and explosive population growth, soaring from just a few hundred to nearly 5,000.

Area settlers watched the development around them with interest. These were hard working and conservative people, but the boom must have seemed a sure thing to them, since some put their own money into mill town developments, like early settlers Harry French and Ed Church, who invested in a brick building on Market Street.

North of Kirkland, on Juanita Bay, Dorr Forbes was busy logging Finn Hill and operating a shingle mill on Juanita Creek. At that time the bay was substantially larger, separating Juanita from Kirkland. Forbes believed that Juanita property values would rise if it was more accessible. Knowing a canal link with the Sound was inevitable, Forbes and others saw Juanita Bay as a future shipping center when the steel mill got off the ground. Forbes believed he was in the right place at the right time.

To connect Juanita to Kirkland, Forbes built his own one-half mile causeway, to bridge the bay that then separated Juanita and Kirkland. There were no pesky government regulations or permits to worry about, he just whacked down some trees, slid them down to his mill, finished them into timbers and started building. When he was done a fine span crossed the bay, linking Juanita and Kirkland.

Even though Juanita Bay never became a shipping center, Forges' bridge was an important improvement that brought more people into Juanita. A pier jutted from the bridge and served as a steamer dock. Years later, Dorr Forbes' son, Les, built a small waiting structure and confectionery business on the steamer pier, which he operated with his wife, Alicia (Stuart). The lake level was lowered by nine feet in 1916 when the Montlake Cut was completed, and Juanita Bay became too shallow for steamers, and the business closed.

Forbes' bridge lasted until 1932, when the current bridge—now exclusively for foot traffic—was opened. There is no remaining evidence of the steamer pier. The old pilings rising from the lake, misidentified by historical markers, are actually from a dock built to accommodate sand and gravel barges decades after Dorr Forbes built his bridge to the boomtown that, like may pioneers, he'd hoped Kirkland would soon become.

Robert, Lucy, and son Don Barrie (armed with a toy rifle) on the old Juanita Bridge, during the 1910s.

Looking north, prior to the 1916 lake lowering, along Forbes' bridge. A commercial dock extended from the west side of the structure.

Facing south, a better look at the bridge, left, and the Juanita Dock with its structures. Though originally established by Harry Langdon, brothers Allen and Les Forbes (with his wife Alicia) ran a small store on the dock that also served as a steamer landing.

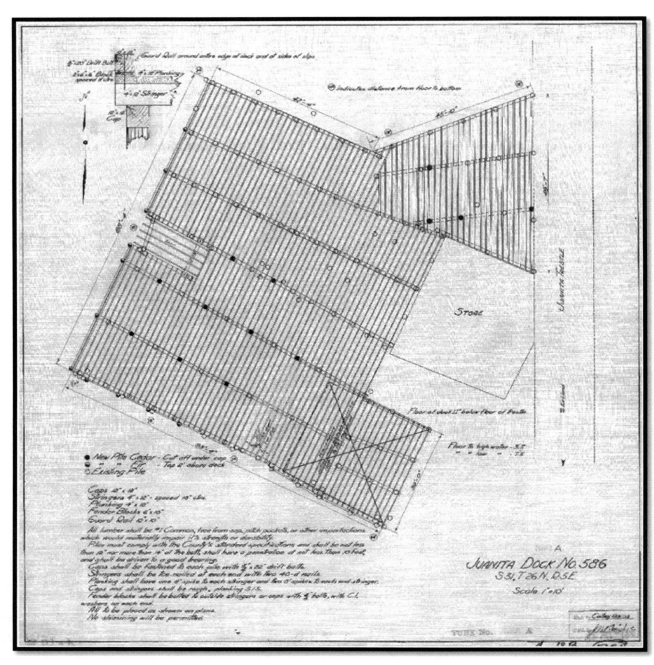

These plans were for an early 1900s Juanita Dock improvement project.

This early view of Juanita Bay with the bridge in the background, faces east. Juanita Bay was for many years associated with logging activities. Here, loggers remove logs from the lake at the site of today's Juanita Bay Park.

This view faces south. A gravel pit located on the Josten homestead, the site of today's Juanita High School, provided gravel for area road surfacing. Gravel barges used the dock extending from the old Juanita bridge

Juanita pioneer and entrepreneur Harry Langdon realized early on that the automobile was here to stay, so he opened a very early commercial garage and gas station at the northern end of the bridge, just visible at extreme right.

167

The old pier remains that today reach into Juanita Bay were not associated with the bay's steamboat days. It is all that's left of a 1920s-era dock for gravel scows used by the City of Seattle. (Photo by Matthew W McCauley)

1921: L.L. Forbes Builds a Bathing Beach at Juanita

Juanita Beach's first bathhouse, built in 1921. Juanita Beach began as a private business venture, established by L. L. "Les" Forbes, the son of Juanita pioneers.

Swimming with my sister and cousins at Juanita Beach as a small boy in the late 1960's is one of my earliest childhood memories. An out-of-the-way King County park for over a decade, it had seemed much older. The rotting remains of wooden groins still protruded from the beach and mysterious, weathered old pilings rose from the lake. On the eastern edge, timeworn vacation cabins stood behind a rusted chain link fence, like a ghost town. Twenty-five years later, an interview with Dorris (Forbes) Beecher solved my boyhood mystery.

According to Dorris, the old shoreline reached today's Juanita Drive prior to the nine-foot lake lowering in 1916. Juanita pioneers Dorr and Eliza Forbes' house still stands—at 11829 N.E. 97th St.—and their son, Les, and daughter-in-law, Alicia, (Dorris Beecher's parents) lived nearby. The Forbes' land adjoined the lake. Dorr had used it to store logs during his lumbering days in the late 1800s.

In 1916, the lake level dropped, gradually uncovering considerable 'new' land at shallow Juanita Bay. The Forbes family was delighted with what they found in their new backyard: the receding water revealed a beautiful, vast expanse of sand beach at Juanita Bay's north side, sand that had been deposited, over millennia, by Juanita Creek.

Word of the sandy beach, a rarity on Lake Washington, spread quickly. From miles away people trekked to the beach to swim and picnic. Dorr died in 1919 (from complications of a simple hernia operation), but in 1920 Les and his partner, Ed Nelson, opened a small concession counter, serving bathers who happened by. In 1921, Les bought a strip of waterfront land from his mother and two additional strips, giving him the eastern 100 feet of today's park site.

There was much work to be done. The beach was strewn with logs—sinkers from pre-1916 log storage days—and, lacking herd laws, livestock wandered the new beach leaving hoof prints and other evidence of grazing. Using horses, Les and Alicia cleared the logs and cleaned the place up. Then they built a small bathhouse and officially opened their new business: L. L. Forbes Juanita Beach.

In the 1920s Les Forbes attached these cards to the radiator caps of his paid customers' cars. Locals could always tell when the beach had been busy—these cards were strewn along the roadway.

Before the lake was lowered, Les and Alicia ran a small confectionery business at the Juanita Bay steamboat dock, off the Juanita Bridge. This photo of the couple with their young daughter, Dorris, dates from about 1915. Note the advertising sign suspended about the Juanita Bridge behind them.

Alicia, Dorris, Joyce, and Les Forbes pose across the road from their beach. The slightly out-of-focus structure behind them is where Spud's Fish & Chips stands today—at 9702 N.E. Juanita Drive.

1922: L.L. and Alicia Forbes and the Beaches at Juanita.

L. L. Forbes Juanita Beach in 1927. Hot summer days drew thousands of bathers to the three privately operated beaches that operated at the site of today's Juanita Beach Park.

In 1922, their second year operating Juanita Beach, Les and Alicia Forbes enlarged their bathhouse and added a plank walkway to help bathers knock the sand off their feet. They continued what would be a long series of improvements in 1923 by converting their home—located across the street—into a lunch counter and light grocery store. The barren beach needed shade, so the couple planted 150 quick-growing cottonwood trees they had barged in from Houghton. Many of these trees still stand.

They developed their beach incrementally, adding an open air kitchen in 1925, swimming suit rentals in 1927, and a large two-story bathhouse and dance hall in 1928. They built a long pier stretching far into the bay, with a boat house offering canoe, sail, and motorboat rentals.

Originally, admission was free, their profits coming from store sales and picnic table rentals (25 cents). Customers re-renting the tables became a problem, so they began charging admission by the carload. This led to customers arriving in several cars and then all piling into one to get in for the sale carload price. Finally, Les Forbes switched a single, 10-cent per-head admission. This change prompted some customer grumbling, but they soon got used to it and the business' revenues increased.

Juanita Beach drew crowds but it never made Les and Alicia rich. Liability insurance was expensive, even then, and Washington's season-limiting weather ensured the beach was no more than a second-income operation, weekends only for Les. He worked during the week as a clerk for Judge Rhea Whitehead. Alicia, with their five children, ran the beach on weekdays. Dorris (Forbes) Beecher described her parents as hard working people who often skimped in order to provide for their children's educations. Several—including Mrs. Beecher—graduated from the University of Washington or other institutions of higher education. She said Alicia was ahead of her time, at least for the Eastside, as the first woman in the area to bob her hair—a daring cut in Juanita during the 1920s. She is quick to point out, however, that Alicia, a well respected community leader, was definitely *not* a flapper.

Competition was another factor in the Roaring 20s. While L. L. Forbes Juanita Beach was the eastern third of today's park, two other adjoining private beaches, Shady Beach and Sandy Beach, occupied the rest. Imported gumwood diving boards, deluxe cooking shelters, and elaborate, high water slides were among the amenities beach operators used to draw customers away from competitors.

Shady Beach concession stand, about 1930.

View of Juanita Beach from the gravel wharf. Its bathhouse was a prominent landmark.

Little Milton Sessions enjoys Juanita Beach, c. 1926.

Juanita Beach founders Les and Alicia Forbes, married for over 50 years, in 1960.

1920s: The Juanita Beach Cabins

Juanita Beach Cabins in the 1920s. Located east of Juanita Beach, the cabins were popular with Seattle families who wanted the experience of then-remote Juanita . The cabins stood until the 1970s when a condominium was built on the site.

Business boomed at Juanita's three privately operated beaches in the 1920s. In keeping with South Juanita's beach resort theme, the Juanita Beach Cabins were constructed adjacent to L.L. Forbes Juanita Beach. Although the Forbes family did not own the cabins, Les and his wife, Alicia, leased the business, operating it with their beach, thus joining a string of Forbes family's entrepreneurial pursuits that spanned generations.

Les' father, Dorr, traded livestock in the South immediately after his Civil War service in the Union Army, and later tried cranberry growing after moving here in 1877. Eventually settling into various lumbering activities, he also owned Forbes Dance Hall, among other ventures.

In the 1890s, Dorr took young Les to Alaska where the two sold eggs to gold miners. Years later Awes told his daughter, Dorris (Forbes) Beecher, that he wished he had brought phonograph records to sell because miners wanted the rare cylinders more than eggs and were paying outrageous sums for them.

After the lake lowering forced Les and Alicia to close their store on the Juanita steamer dock in 1916, Les supported his family for a short time by selling the pelts of muskrats he trapped at Juanita Bay.

Many of the beach and cabin patrons came from outside Kirkland. Henry Ford had made the automobile available to most Americans, who loved mobility it delivered. In those days, driving around the lake from Seattle to Juanita was itself an adventure. The cabins were popular with day visitors as well as Seattle families who stayed by the week.

Dorris (Forbes) Beecher said the area's resort-era peaked around 1932. In the 1930s, Juanita Park was built east of the cabins, where the Treasure House store stands today. It was more of an amusement park, offering a dance hall and rides.

As Les and Alicia approached their senior years, they leased their beach out to others and took over the cabin business. In 1956 the couple sold their property, including the family home Les' parents built in 1905, to King County for $46,000. The county also bought the Shady Beach and Sandy Beach properties, which, when combined, created today's Juanita Beach Park. The couple moved to Camano Island, which Les said reminded him of the undeveloped Juanita of his 1890s childhood.

The Juanita Beach Cabins stood until the early 1970s. Interestingly, one survives still survives. A Finn Hill resident, and a friend of my father, drove past the cabins during their demolition and offered the foreman $25 to deliver it to his property. The foreman agreed. The cabin sits on a cinderblock foundation, a few miles from its original site. It is now a sauna.

A matchbook cover from the early years, probably the 1930s.

The inside of the matchbook cover at left.

Juanita Junction, from the air, looking to the south. The Juanita Beach Cabins are at the right, just off Juanita Drive. L.L. Forbes Juanita Beach is adjacent, with its pavilion and dock at the water's edge. Art's Food Center is the larger structure (center). To the left, just west of 100th Avenue, are the charred ruins of Harry Langdon's garage. Just across the street was Roy's Market, a Juanita Junction landmark until the 1970s.

Another view of Juanita Beach and Juanita Beach Cabins, looking northeast

1914: Darius Kinsey Visits the Eastside, Meets Captain Gilbert and *his* Boats.

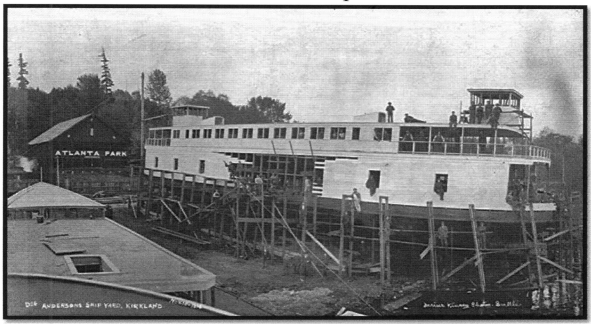

The famous Northwest photographer Darius Kinsey visited Kirkland in 1914. While here he took many photographs of area schools, people, and industries. Many of his subjects bought his prints (it was how he made his living) and some of those prints are still in senior Kirklanders' hands, like this one, which came from *A Look to the Past* reader's attic.

The above photo is dated Nov. 10, 1914 and depicts Anderson Shipyard workers, with the steam ferry *Lincoln* and passenger steamer *Dawn* under construction. John Anderson's Atlanta Park dance pavilion is seen in the background. Senior Kirklanders remember the *Lincoln* well. She ran regularly on the Kirkland-Madison Park route from her launching, in December 1914.

During World War II she made special runs carrying workers to the shipyard. Most of her crew lived in or near Kirkland. One of the boat's engineers, Herb Brooks, made the newspaper after building an amazingly accurate, 22-inch metal model of the vessel that was exact in every detail. The *Lincoln* was eventually replaced by the *Leschi*. The *Lincoln* was taken out of the lake, and sold for salvage in the 1950s.

The little 65-foot *Dawn*, in the foreground, was built to replace the old *Cyrene* on the west Mercer Island run, and was originally powered by the steam engine removed from the early lake steamer *Xanthus*. She would play an important part in the life of Frank Gilbert, one young worker seen in the photo.

Gilbert was a Kirkland resident whose father, Elmer E. Gilbert, had owned a Kirkland blacksmith shop and livery stable as well as the Hotel Gilbert. Frank didn't like blacksmithing, but he did like boats, so he hired on with Anderson. He not only helped build the *Lincoln* and the *Dawn,* but shortly after returning from service in World War I became the skipper of the 250-passenger, 75-ton *Dawn.* He remained at her helm for 22 years. There, for his entire tenure, Gilbert worked the 5:30 pm to 1:30 am shift, until she was retired in 1938. Island resident Sven Hanson ran the boat during the mornings and early afternoons. The *Dawn* served primarily on the Leschi-Mercer Island west side foot passenger route, and to many senior islanders she was a much-loved little vessel.

In a 1961 *Mercer Island Reporter* newspaper article, long-time Mercer Island resident Virginia Ogden Elliott recalled the *Dawn* during the 1920s, "Inside, the Dawn was divided, like all Gaul, into three parts. The inside cabin for the women, children and transient travelers; the outside and upper decks for the teenagers, and the engine room for the men. The engine room, which was on the way to the cabin, had benches around both sides of the engine, and behind the boxed-in warm boiler. These seats were the men's property and smoking section—no woman was bold enough to smoke on the boat in those days. Most of the affairs on the Island were settled in the warm, oil-smelling, smoke-filled little room. It was transportation and city hall. Our fathers sat in a certain irrevocable order on the long benches and we remember with amusement one of them standing reading his paper, glancing up—perhaps glaring—until the offender took the hint and moved to another seat. They were in the same seats every day."

Skipper Gilbert had no crew but himself, and he performed all functions as well, from handling the freight to collecting the fares. Islanders addressed him with affection simply as "Capt'n Frank." When the Lacy Murrow Floating Bridge opened in 1940, connecting Seattle to Mercer Island and the eastside, car ferry and steamer service to Mercer Island was no longer needed. Gilbert went on to captain the *Leschi* with other Kirkland-area crew members, some of whom Gilbert had known since his childhood.

Post-retirement, the *Dawn* was sold to a private party and tied up at Rainier Beach where her machinery was scrapped and she ingloriously sank at her moorings. She became a safety hazard. In 1941 she was scuttled in the lake and today rests under 110 feet of water off of Rainier Beach. She is now a great SCUBA dive for those willing to brave the lake's cold, dark depths. Though her upper deck was removed when her steam engine was extracted, she is almost intact. Up through the 1980s her wreckage contained brass hinges, fittings and other mementos that were originally affixed by Gilbert and the other highly skilled craftsmen seen in Kinsey's photograph on the previous page.

In this 1900s view, looking north, Market Street is visible behind the Bank Building at left. Center left is Elmer Gilbert's blacksmith shop and his Hotel Gilbert is up on the bluff, right. His son Frank chose a career on the lake instead of either of these enterprises.

Though Elmer E. Gilbert owned several Kirkland enterprises in the 1900s, his son Frank chose to make Lake Washington steamboats his career. At right, Captain Frank Gilbert at the *Leshi's* helm in 1946.

The venerable, Houghton-built *Dawn* served Mercer Island residents for decades and is still fondly remembered. She was one of the toughest, most seaworthy vessels on the lake. Stripped of her engine and upper deck, she was scuttled. She rests on the floor of the lake.

Elmer and Jennie Gilbert, Captain Frank Gilbert's parents, came to Kirkland from Pennsylvania in 1889 during the steel mill boom years. They remained after the crash. Highly entrepreneurial, Gilbert at various times was involved in several early Kirkland businesses. (Photo and information courtesy of Anita Maxwell)

The colorful Leigh S. J. Hunt was described by a contemporary as "A financier and businessman of very unusual talents." He convinced Peter Kirk that the new steel mill should be located on Lake Washington and of the Eastside's potential as a future steel manufacturing and shipping area.

Contrary to common belief, Peter Kirk didn't invent Kirkland. Leigh Hunt did. Leigh S.J. Hunt (1855-1933) wanted to win friends, influence people, and on the way, amass a fortune. So he moved from Indiana to Washington, and on November 1, 1886, he bought the *Seattle Post-Intelligencer,* then Seattle's most popular newspaper.

According to Arline Ely's *Our Foundering Fathers*—probably the best-researched published account of the Kirkland's steel mill days—fortunes were made overnight in the West, and Hunt wanted in on the action. Washington Territory offered enormous opportunity for budding "Robber Barons." Timber, mineral, and agricultural resources were waiting to be exploited and Hunt bought the *Post Intelligencer* to promote the various ventures he planned. By all accounts he was a promoter extraordinaire.

Then considered the law-and-order newspaper—for example, its previous owners had opposed Seattle's anti-Chinese riots—Hunt used the *Post Intelligencer* to his advantage and soon became one of the area's most politically influential figures. Pretty good for a 31-year-old.

Hunt and his wife preferred the Eastside to Seattle and bought land on all three points: Evergreen, Yarrow, and Hunt's, which was named for him. The Hunts lived in a large estate at the tip of Yarrow Point. His western view from his home was obscured by tall trees on Hunt's Point, so he bought it and had the trees removed.

Hunt met Peter Kirk, who was looking for a site for his steel mill, and persuaded Kirk to locate the mill at the site of the village that became Kirkland. To convert iron ore into steel requires three raw materials: iron ore; coke, made from coal and burned as a smelting heat source; and limestone, a flux in separating impurities.

Kirk had a master's grasp of the technical aspects of the art and science of steel manufacturing. His focus had been on locating the mill where it was most efficient to transport the raw materials. He had considered the Tacoma area for its proximity to the Wilkeson-Carbonado coal mines and he came close the locating the enterprise at Sallal Prairie, a small mining town near today's North Bend, for its proximity to iron ore and limestone sources around Snoqualmie Pass. Coking coal would come from the Black Diamond area.

But Hunt was the salesman, not Kirk. While Kirk wanted to manufacture steel rails, Hunt wanted to create an empire. His vision included not only the steel mill itself, but huge profits derived from developing the land, town site, and ancillary industries where the mill was to be located.

"The possibilities are endless," Hunt told Kirk. Hunt helped bring other prominent Seattle businessmen, including Seattle co-founder A. A. Denny, into their corporation. By 1888, they were off and running, and Kirkland became a boom town. The Seattle fire of 1889 brought financial challenges. After a corporate reorganization, the salesman Hunt brought in capital from savvy out-of-state financiers.

But fortunes built on speculation could be lost overnight. The Panic of 1893 hit Hunt very hard. He was wiped out financially and deeply in debt, so he handed his newspaper and property over to his creditors and left town.

Undaunted by his financial troubles, which included bankruptcy, Hunt traveled to Asia and became the first white man to enter North Korea, where his drive and perseverance paid off. There he opened gold mines, and later he irrigated part of the Sudan, and developed the first cotton plantation on the White Nile.

Later he returned to Seattle, and for two days ran an advertisement asking his old creditors to visit his hotel room. He repaid every dime he owed—with interest. Jim Collins, son of Kirkland's first mayor, R. H. Collins, who had come to Kirkland in 1890, described Leigh Hunt as "A financier and businessman of very unusual talents."

Hunt died on October 5, 1933. His doctors had suggested he move to a dry climate. He chose a small Nevada railroad station town, which he promoted, hoping to build it into a great city, an oasis in the desert. It was a whistle stop called Las Vegas.

This section of steel rail is on display at the Resource Center of the Kirkland Heritage Society, at the lower level of Heritage Hall, 203 Market Street. It was manufactured at Peter Kirk's Moss Bay Hematite iron & Steel Company, of Workington, England, shipped around Cape Horn (southern tip of South America) to Seattle where it was used by the Seattle Lake Shore & Eastern Railroad for its line connecting Seattle to Woodinville.

One of the original group of Seattle settlers, Arthur Armstrong Denny (1822-99) helped finance Leigh Hunt's steel mill. He came to Puget Sound from Illinois by covered wagon in 1851, and served in Washington's Territorial Legislature and in the 39th U.S. Congress in 1865-67. A vigorous booster of the Seattle business community, Denny was involved in banking, milling, merchandising, irrigation projects, street railways, and was a chief legislative sponsor and land donor for the creation of the University of Washington. Denny's Snoqualmie Pass mines were to have supplied iron ore to the Kirkland steel mill.

1912, 1994: *John Wester and Sue Carter's Incredible, Once-Ubiquitous House*

The house once belonging to Sue Carter, built by former Kirkland Mayor John Wester, stood on Third Street from 1912 until 2008.

Located on the hill, behind Kirkland's city hall, on Third Avenue, the ubiquitous Sue Carter house seems to be lurking in the background of just about every post-1912 photograph of downtown Kirkland. Both inside and out it is still remarkably similar to its original form, while the surrounding area has experienced enormous changes.

Kirkland boasts numerous historic homes, especially in the neighborhoods near City Hall and west of Market Street and all seem to have fascinating histories. While many were built by Kirk's Kirkland Land and Improvement Company, Carter's house, which has been her home for decades, serves as an interesting example of housing from the post-Kirk years.

Walking into her well maintained house feels like you've just walked into 1913, the year the house was built. The design is intriguing and the craftsmanship evident in the painstaking detail of the woodwork, prompting the question, "Who built this house?" John Wester built it.

His name may not be a familiar name in Kirkland anymore, but he left numerous lasting reminders of his time in Kirkland.

A 1933 newspaper story reported, "Judging from his list of activities since he came to Kirkland in 1912 we would judge that John has either superintended, designed, or built about half of Kirkland. He ain't got a barrel o' money but he has the respect and admiration of all his fellow men."

Wester, a building contractor, served as Kirkland's mayor and the Kirkland Chamber of Commerce's president. He designed and built dozens of Kirkland homes and many old downtown buildings, including Burke and Farrar, Wickencamp, J.C. Penney, the Journal Building, National Supply, Ford Blau, and the old junior high. He built much of the Lake Street South block which recently suffered a tragic arson fire (ironically, when first completed, buildings there were proclaimed fireproof).

Wester was elected mayor unanimously in 1926. Although popular, he declined a second term writing in 1929, "...the time and effort demanded by position means too great a sacrifice to my family and business...I am sure experience of the past years has made me...a more firm believer in the ultimate future of this wonderful community."

(**2010 Update**: the City of Kirkland purchased the home from Sue Carter for a possible City Hall expansion. Carter relocated and the city rented the home to tenants for several years. The house, needed substantial repairs, and given the high costs associated with refurbishment and upkeep on a structure slated for possible removal, the city opted to demolish the house in 2008).

John Wester, mayor of Kirkland, and builder.

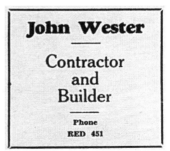

Wester (1880 – 1949) constructed many of Kirkland's best remembered commercial buildings and homes.

Many structures built by John Wester were occupied by companies with a long residence in Kirkland.

One of the first photos of Sue Carter's house, seen between 1912 and 1916. This shot faces north from the ferry dock and provides a rare view of the old lake level and sparse development along today's Lake Street South and Central Way. At the top of the next page is another look from the same time period, this one was taken from a boat. The Sue Carter house is visible just behind the old Gilbert Hotel at the right. The old Central School is in the center and Bank Building is left, behind the Standard Mill dock at the foot of Market Street.

Looking up Lake Street South in this early view, the Carter house is alone on the hill. It witnessed nearly a century of development as the small town began to grow.

And the town did grow...

STREET SCENE - KIRKLAND - Wash

...and grow...

...and grow, from a small town to a small city.

And eventually it grew into a thriving, modern city.

Marina Park and the parking lot behind it were under water before the Montlake Cut caused the lake level to lower nine feet. Looking north, Sue Carter's house is visible above the building on the left.

By 2008 the house John Wester built, in which Sue Carter lived for 25 years, was nearly swallowed by ever-denser development. It is barely visible between apartment buildings in the above photo. (Photo Courtesy Dale and Loita Hawkinson)

The end came for the house that had seen so much and witnessed Kirkland evolve from a storybook small town populated by a few hundred souls, to a full-fledged city of nearly 50,000. (Photo by Dale and Lolita Hawkinson)

Sue Carter, upper left, in 1968, with her daughters Carol, middle left, and Nancy, lower left. Evelyn Lanham, right, former Kirkland mayor Lee Lanham's wife. The women were discussing the Forward Thrust bond issues, which included a vast array of improvements including arterial highways, a stadium (this became the Kingdome), parks, and youth service.

1922: Sand Point Naval Air Station and why WWII Combat Warplanes Lie Submerged in Lake Washington

Once a bustling naval flight facility, Naval Air Station (NAS) Seattle at Sand Point was decommissioned for flight operations in 1973 and the US Navy signed the last of its Sand Point facilities over to the City of Seattle in 1995.

Sand Point. You can see it from just about any part of Kirkland. It's our closest western neighbor, and engineers once considered joining it to Kirkland by the bridge that eventually went to Evergreen Point. But to many Kirklanders, Sand Point still brings to mind the roar of propeller-driven aircraft, from its years as Naval Air Station Seattle.

Shortly after World War I, the King County board of commissioners purchased Sand Point and deeded it the federal government at no cost. Congress agreed to build the air station there, a Navy base at Bremerton, and an Army base at Camp Lewis, as it was called then.

Construction at Sand Point began in 1922, which was considered a boon to the Kirkland economy. Workers cut a small airstrip out from the woods and erected a six-plane hangar. Aviation was still in its infancy and military attack planes were little more than armed, motorized kites.

From its humble origins, NAS Seattle grew through the 1930s, but World War II turned the sleepy peacetime base into a bustling hive of activity. While its primary mission was training, planes from Sand Point would have been used to repel any Japanese invasion of the Northwest. Tension was high then, especially since Japanese subs were torpedoing ships within sight of Washington's coast.

Just about every type of naval propeller-driven aircraft flew from Sand Point at one time or another. Some Navy aviators trained on Privateer and Harpoon bombers saw service in the Aleutians, while fighter pilots flew their Wildcats and Hellcats from the aircraft carriers and primitive airstrips carved from the jungles of sweltering South Pacific islands.

After World War II and the Korean War, the base served as a reserve and training facility. By then, the Navy was converting to jet aircraft, which Sand Point's runway was too short to accommodate. The NAS was decommissioned as a flight facility in 1973 and the Navy abandoned its presence there.

But frozen in time, on the lake's dark, cold floor, lasting reminders of World War II sit in an underwater museum of sorts. At least seven US Navy planes, which crashed or ditched in the lake, remain on the bottom. Their radial engines quiet, their machine guns rusted, they still sit in tribute to the brave men who flew them and the generation who sacrificed their youth and innocence to secure our freedom.

The first hangar, erected in 1922.

Chance Vought F4U Corsair fighters. Many based at NAS Seattle at Sand Point were built by the Goodyear Company and designated FG-1D. Two of these aircraft lost during post-war flight operations were salvaged from the lake during the 1980s. Also during that decade author McCauley befriended a number of World War II Corsair pilots who said they loved these planes, describing them as pilot-friendly and nearly indestructible. In Korea they provided ground support and were a welcome sight to marines as they attacked North Korean and Chinese positions.

Prop-driven combat aircraft, like this US Navy PB4Y-2 Privateer, were once a regular sight across the lake from Kirkland. One of these planes crashed into the lake in August, 1956, and still rests upright on the lake floor about 155 feet deep. On the next page is a high resolution side scan sonar image of that plane created by local sonar expert Crayton Fenn of Fenn Enterprises. In a botched 1956 salvage attempt, the US Navy ripped away both inboard engines and nacelles.

An image of a PB4Y Privateer (BuNo 59695) on the bottom of Lake Washington, created by a side-scan sonar (Image Courtesy of Fenn Enterprises, fennent.com). Prop-driven combat aircraft, like this US Navy PB4Y-2 Privateer, were once a regular sight across the lake from Kirkland. This plane crashed into the lake in August, 1956 and still rests in an upright position on the lake floor about 155 feet below the surface. The high-resolution side scan sonar image shown above was created by local sonar expert Crayton Fenn of Fenn Enterprises. In a botched 1956 salvage attempt, the US Navy ripped away both inboard engines and engine nacelles.

Author Matthew W. McCauley, at a Sand Point boat ramp in 1984, salvaging a World War II Curtiss SB2C Helldiver/A-25 Shrike dive bomber from 150 feet beneath the lake surface. The recovery prompted a lawsuit by the US Navy against McCauley and diving partner Jeff Hummel (in the water behind the plane) but the two prevailed in US District Court. The plane was sold and is still undergoing restoration in an Ohio air museum. (Photo by David I. Blair)

199

Author Matthew W. McCauley, right, looks on as Seattle-native and longtime Mercer Island resident Richard "Dick" Hummel shares photographs during an August, 2010 Lake Washington Seafair cruise. Mr. Hummel served in the US Navy during World War II, including duty at NAS Seattle at Sand Point. Post war, he had a lengthy career at Boeing. In the 1970s, Mr. Hummel's first-hand accounts of World War II aircraft lost in Lake Washington fired the imaginations of two teenaged SCUBA divers: his son, Jeff, and McCauley who, with help from other SCUBA-trained friends, went on to salvage from deep water the remains of a total of five World War II era Naval combat aircraft from Lake Washington during the 1980. Three were Curtiss SB2C Helldiver/A-25 Shrike dive bombers and two were Grumman F4F Wildcat fighters. (Photo by Jacob McCauley)

December 7, 1941: WAR!

In World War II many Kirkland women became Rosie-the-riveter industrial workers to support the war effort.

On Sunday morning Dec. 7, 1941, a Japanese fleet bombed Pearl Harbor and awakened not only a sleeping giant but also the sleepy little towns of Kirkland and Houghton. The rural villages soon became bustling centers of activity, especially at the Lake Washington Shipyards, which were at Houghton.

University of Washington history professor and Houghton resident Lorraine McConaghy , wrote her 1987 master's degree thesis, *The Lake Washington Shipyards: For the Duration* about Kirkland's war years. Her extensively researched document provides a fascinating glimpse into how rapidly the war changed the Eastside.

In 1939, the Lake Washington Shipyards employed 250 employees, according to McConaghy. She called the prewar workers the "aristocrats of their trade," often working in their family traditions that spanned generations. Through apprenticeships, workers climbed the ranks in the shipyards, although frequent work shortages between the shipyards contracts, forced many to find work in other trades, such as building furniture and the "stump ranching," by which families supplemented their incomes, by raising livestock and produce on their land.

Wartime mobilization dramatically changed life in Kirkland and at the shipyard. By 1943, nearly 8,000 workers were employed at the shipyard, McConaghy wrote, a huge increase over 1939 employment levels. The flood of workers into the area caused severe housing shortages, sewer problems, and other service difficulties. However, there were also enormous employment opportunities.

By this time, veteran workers were outnumbered by the less-skilled wartime laborers. For the first time, women worked at manual labor at the shipyard, leaving the office behind where most would have been employed in administrative and office jobs before the war. Before December 7, 1941, there were few black people living in Kirkland, and the war opened employment opportunities for black people as well.

Another new arrival, and the target of much ridicule, were the "Okies" and "Arkies," poor white migrants from the rural south and the Midwest.

Though many had survived dustbowl drought—which was vividly depicted by John Steinbeck in *The Grapes of Wrath*— they were nonetheless the butt of many jokes. I have a soft spot for them. One Okie, dustbowl refugee couple who came to the Seattle area for work just after the war were William F. and Oleta Mae "Jeri" McCauley, my grandparents.

Lakeview Terrace was one of several wartime housing developments. This was a child care area at Lakeview Terrace.

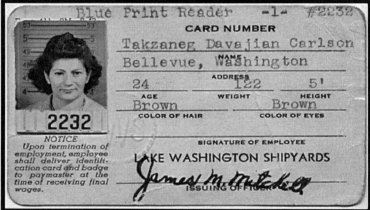

Artifacts of civilian life in war-time Kirkland.

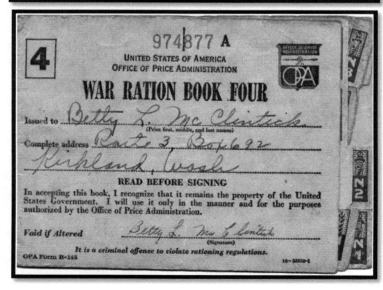

Like many early residents, Houghton settlers Frank and Molly Curtis enjoyed playing musical instruments. Nineteenth century Kirklanders had little trouble entertaining themselves during their free time.

When speaking to groups of children about the history of Kirkland, they often ask me, "What did people around here do for fun back in those days?"

Of course, these kids are trying to imagine a world with no television, radio, video games, CD players, or any of the electronic entertainment devices we accept as part of our lives. While I can't answer from personal experience—I'm 29 and a member of the TV generation member—the journals of senior citizens, newspapers, and interviews with long-time residents can provide insights into how Kirklanders spent their time before the electronic age.

In the above photograph, Houghton settlers Frank and Molly Curtis pose in their home with some of their musical instruments. The Curtises were especially musical, but most families of their day enjoyed playing instruments and singing together or at such gatherings with their neighbors.

Often, as with the Curtises, large families were like small bands, with each member playing a different instrument. Molly Curtis became a popular piano instructor and even taught piano at the University of Washington, then located in downtown Seattle. The Curtis home was the second frame house built in the Kirkland area and many settlers' children took lessons from her there. The photo was taken by Houghton's first permanent settler, Harry French, one of the few Eastsiders who, in the 1880s, owned a camera and engaged in photography as a hobby. Home interior shots are uncommon, but this rare view also shows that someone in the Curtis family enjoyed painting, another favorite activity then.

Adults and children made the best of their free time. Rural life was demanding and labor was a big part of life, even for youngsters who had chores each day. Sometimes fun activities also helped the family. Berry picking, hunting, and fishing all helped put food on the table.

Darkness forced evening activities indoors. Such activities included writing letters, keeping journals, and of course reading books and newspapers. Books and newspapers could be hard to come by, so individual volumes and issues were often shared throughout the community.

While work occupied Monday through Saturday, most settlers did not to work on Sundays, and most attended church services. After that, they often enjoyed a community activity such as an afternoon picnic or time at home with families.

The Curtis House, built in 1883, and the Curtis family, from the left: Frank, Walt, Alvin, and Molly.

Houghton's pioneering Fish and Kirtley families and others enjoy an outing to Snoqualmie Falls. In the late nineteenth century, the Seattle Lake Shore & Eastern Railway provided rail service between Kirkland, the falls, and beyond to North Bend.

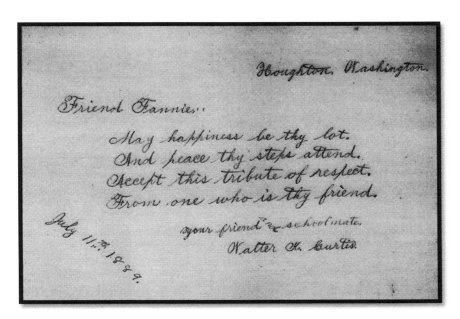

Walt Curtis (1874-1945) wrote this to Fanny Kirk (1876-1956) in her autograph book. Fanny was Peter and Mary Kirk's daughter. If young Walt was trying to impress her he may have blown it by misspelling her name.

1933: The Kalakala, the Northwest's Most Famous Streamlined Ferry.

The Northwest's most famous ferry, the *Kalakala*, was constructed in Houghton during the 1930s from the remains of a burned San Francisco Bay ferry.

On May 6, 1933, the "fireproof and unsinkable" San Francisco Bay ferry *Peralta* burned in a spectacular fire at the Oakland terminal. Although her hull, designed by Hibbs, McCauley, & Smith, remained relatively sound, her entire superstructure was destroyed.

Her owners were happy to sell her remains to the Northwest's Black Ball Line, which towed the hulk north, to Puget Sound and then into Houghton's Lake Washington Shipyards. When she reached local waters few people would have believed that the pile of scrap would be rebuilt and reborn the *Kalakala*, the most recognized ferry on the West Coast

Once moored at the Lake Washington Shipyard, workers removed her engines and the wreckage that had been her superstructure. They narrowed the main deck from 70 to 56 feet and Black Ball's owner, Captain Alex Peabody, called for an entirely new superstructure arrangement for 1,500 passengers.

It was this modern, streamlined, steel superstructure that immortalized the *Kalakala*. The streamlined design had been subjected to wind velocity and other tests by Boeing engineers, not a common practice in shipbuilding at the time. It was also an out-of-the-ordinary job for the Lake Washington Shipyard's general manager Paul Voinot, who had to devise numerous special construction methods.

Her trial run, on July 2, 1935, drew world-wide media attention and more than 100,000 spectators. She began her regular service schedule shortly after, running between Seattle and Bremerton during the day. On summer evenings, she made excursion trips around the sound. She boasted her own eight-piece orchestra, "The Flying Birds," and dancing on three decks. Her interior appointments were impressive and many people remember her horseshoe shaped lunch counter.

She was undoubtedly the most photographed vessel in Washington's history. Post cards, paintings and souvenir materials depicted the *Kalakala* cruising on Elliott Bay against the background of Seattle's skyline.

The *Kalakala*—which translates to "flying bird" in Chinook language—operated on the sound until 1967. When her maintenance and fuel costs became too large for economical operations, she was retired. She was sold for $100,000 to American Freezerships, towed to Alaska, and sits at a beach near Kodiak today. She houses a fish processing plant.

(**2010 Update**—The *Kalakala* drama has taken many twists and turns since I wrote this column in 1994. The vessel was recovered from the beach in Alaska and returned to Washington in 1998. Since that time she has been moored at Lake Union and Neah Bay and is currently tied up in Tacoma. Her current owner, Steve Rodrigues, estimates that restoration will cost $15 million. Her future is uncertain).

2010 view, the once-beloved vessel moored at Tacoma awaiting her fate.

1860: Mr. Peter Kirk of Messrs Kirk Bros. & Co. Ltd., and other Enterprises.

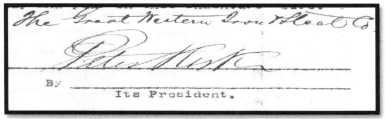

Peter Kirk (1840-1916)

An early 1920s *East Side Journal* letter to the editor argued for replacing Kirkland's street names. He didn't like the fact that they commemorated places in England like Picadilly Street, Fleet Street, and Waverly Way. He reminded readers that the names had been chosen by "a certain Englishman who spent some time in these parts a while back." Kirklanders rejected the malcontent's suggestions. They liked their quaint street names, and despite the economic catastrophe resulting from his efforts, Peter Kirk is remembered fondly around the now grown-up city that bears his name.

Myths about Kirk still abound. Some people insist that he lived in the red brick Creative Arts/Peter Kirk Building, on Market Street—he didn't, he lived in various houses—or that he was one of those rich, ruling-class, 19th century Brits who had never done a lick of work in his life and simply came here to throw money around. That was wrong as well.

Arline Ely's, *Our Foundering Fathers*, though long out of print, remains about the best researched works available about Kirkland's Kirk years. She reported that Kirk was one of three brothers who moved to Workington, England from their family home in a Derbyshire. Though the family iron manufacturing and founding business was moderately successful, it was not enough to support the three brothers, so they struck out on their own.

In 1860 they acquired a small forge and opened Kirk Brothers & Co. Ltd, which enjoyed moderate success. But Peter was more ambitious than that. He left the family business, and, at age 27, went into partnership with his brother-in-law in Moss Bay Hermite Iron and Steel, Ltd, which grew to employ more than 1,000 men making steel rails, which were shipped worldwide. Kirk was an expert in the business, and invented machinery and processes for making steel. He held a number of patents, probably the most significant being his 1884 design for metal railroad ties, which the English called sleepers.

Ely described Kirk as a thin man of average height, with brown hair, who carried himself in a mannerly and hospitable fashion. He was an avid reader and he enjoyed playing the organ and composing music. He was married to Mary Ann (Quirk) Kirk, and by the time the Kirk family immigrated to America, in 1888, the couple had seven living children.

Mary Ann (Quirk) Kirk (1840-1907)

MESSRS. KIRK BROTHERS & CO.,

Ironmasters and Manufacturers,

NEW YARD & MARSH SIDE IRON WORKS, WORKINGTON.

The important business indicated above may be said to date from the year 1860, when Messrs. Henry, Thomas, and Peter Kirk purchased the New Yard Forge, which at that time possessed only one forge hammer and two heating furnaces, with the accompanying engines, sheds, and forge buildings. A new rolling mill for medium sized bars was at once erected, and a further steam hammer added to the forge plant in the following year. Encouraged by the success attendant upon these improvements, Messrs. Kirk, in 1863-4, erected two other rolling mills, one for large and one for smaller sizes, at the same time putting down a heavier steam hammer, together with corresponding puddling and heating furnaces. Subsequently a commodious iron and brass foundry was built, this development being followed by the purchase of the rivet factory formerly carried on by Messrs. Dixons. These premises, it may be noted, are situated opposite Messrs. Kirk Brothers and Co.'s general offices on Marsh Side, now mainly utilised

that, in 1880 a blast furnace was started and has been kept in operation ever since, the output consisting of a superior grade of pig iron obtained by the combination of the rich hæmatite ores of the district with other materials in proportions calculated to secure highly satisfactory tensile properties, and maximum degrees of strength, durability, and quality generally. The "new departure" of 1880 has proved of infinite advantage to the firm, for it has enabled them to avail themselves of the abundant natural supplies of hæmatite ore and ironstone within the immediate neighbourhood of their works, thus diminishing the cost of production, and allowing a better and cheaper article to be placed upon the market. As at present organised, Messrs. Kirk Brothers and Co.'s operative resources embrace five rolling mills (two "puddle bar" and three "finishing"), which are capable of a total yield of 600 tons of rough bars and 600 tons of finished bars per week, and pig iron smelting furnace equal to the production of 700 tons of metal per week.

MR. HENRY KIRK.

An English trade journal from the 1870s wrote about Peter Kirk's venture with his brothers in Workington, England. His brother Henry's (1831-1914) likeness was used.

Four of the Kirk Daughters: Hannah Oliver "Olive" (1870-1944) is standing at left, Jessie (1880-1965) is in the middle, Fanny (1874-1956) is in the back on the right and Clara (1878-1946) is kneeling in front. The Kirk's had five daughters and three sons. The other children were Frank (1866-74), Florence (1868-1949), Marie (1872-1904), Peter, Jr (1876-1951) and Arnold (1883-1956).

The hand-written word was much more important in the lives of people before today's era of instant electronic communication.

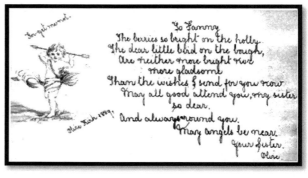

In the ages before modern electronic entertainment and communication, educated people routinely kept diaries and wrote notes or letters.

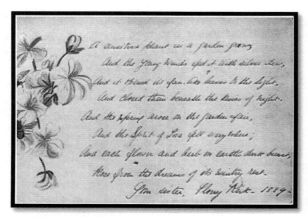

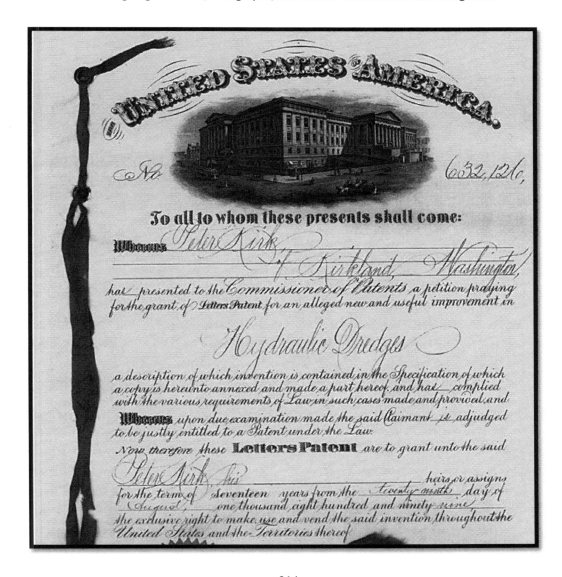

"On a true friend."
Hast thou a Friend? Thou hast indeed a rich and large supply, Treasure to serve your every need, & well managed till you die.

Marie Kirk
Kirkland
Feb 2nd '89.

The foregoing are notes, autographs, and letters related to the Kirk daughters.

UNITED STATES OF AMERICA.

No. 632,126,

To all to whom these presents shall come:

Whereas Peter Kirk of Kirkland, Washington, has presented to the Commissioner of Patents a petition praying for the grant of Letters Patent for an alleged new and useful improvement in

Hydraulic Dredges

a description of which invention is contained in the Specification of which a copy is hereunto annexed and made a part hereof, and has complied with the various requirements of Law in such cases made and provided, and

Whereas upon due examination made the said Claimant is adjudged to be justly entitled to a Patent under the Law.

Now therefore these **Letters Patent** are to grant unto the said

Peter Kirk his heirs or assigns for the term of seventeen years from the twenty-ninth day of August, one thousand eight hundred and ninety-nine, the exclusive right to make, use and vend the said invention throughout the United States and the Territories thereof.

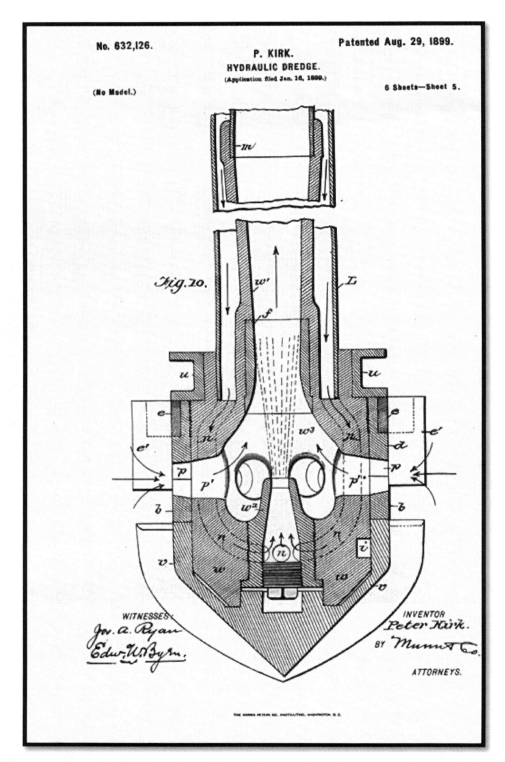

Peter Kirk patented several of his inventions. The two images above, from 1899, relate to a hydraulic dredge. Other Kirk patents included an iron smelter and metal rail ties—called sleepers by the English.

Fir Grove was the Kirk family home in Kirkland, in the 200 block of Waverly Way. After Peter Kirk died in 1916, his sons sold the property to the real estate firm Burke and Farrar, which demolished the house and built two smaller homes on the lot. The Kirkland Heritage Society has in its collection small pieces of the siding and nails from Fir Grove.

The image of Fir Grove also serves as the Kirkland Heritage Society's logo.

1887: A Ride on the Squak

The *Squak* was the first steam boat built on Lake Washington. The *Squak* operated there and on Lake Sammamish. Captain J. F. Curtis (in the wheelhouse doorway), Fanny Kirk, Mrs. J. F. Curtis, Mrs. Kneisel and her daughter, M.L. Baer, Mrs. T. H. Duncan, Maud Frederick, Gertrude Duncan, Ben Wright, Al H. Curtis and T. H. Duncan. In the back row are Olive Kirk and Marie Kirk. The group had just come from a picnic at Juanita Bay and apparently decided to collect some cattails to memorialize the outing. Walt Curtis took this photo, the only known photo of the fondly-remembered vessel.

Prior to 1884, the few small steamers operating on Lake Washington were brought onto the lake by the Black River, which flowed out of the southern end of the lake into Puget Sound. These vessels were originally built for salt water use and their primary function on the lake was to tow coal barges from Newcastle Mine landing to the portage at Union Bay, so they provided Eastside settlers with only sporadic, undependable service. Most people relied on their own muscle-powered rowboats and canoes. Even when they could hire one of the steamers to haul freight, the lack of docks and shallow shoreline water often necessitated unloading cargoes offshore and slogging the load through the water up to the beach.

Captain Jay C. O'Conner changed all that when he had Ed Lee build him the 42-foot, twin screw, steam scow *Squak*, near the site of today's Carillon Point. The *Squak* was the first steam powered vessel built on Lake Washington and her shallow draft, a mere two and a half feet, narrow beam (14 feet), and practical, though awkward looking, design allowed the skipper to run her up onto the beach to offload cargo.

The hull design also enabled her to navigate the twisting, snag-infested Sammamish River, then called Squak Slough, to serve Redmond, and to travel beyond Redmond into Lake Sammamish, then called Squak Lake, and then south to Issaquah—and yes, Issaquah was then called Squak.

Houghton-area resident Wells Green served as her engineer in her first years. His was a critical job, since these crude, early boilers needed a skilled operator to avoid developing too much steam pressure. Over-pressuring a boiler could cause an explosion and kill everyone on a vessel, so skippers always sought talented engineers.

In a 1950s newspaper column, the late Lucile McDonald reported excerpts of a letter from Margaret Yarno, who had traveled to Lake Sammamish on the *Squak* in 1887 to be a bridesmaid at a wedding. McDonald wrote that Yarno said the *Squak* left the McGilvra homestead, near the foot of Seattle's Madison Street, loaded with about 25 loggers bound for Fall City and North Bend.

"The boat was so narrow you could reach out and touch both sides of the cabin. Capt. O'Conner ran it and Wells Green was engineer. We left at 8 a.m. and arrived at Bothell at 2 p.m. I'd had no breakfast and nothing else to eat. Mrs. (David C.) Bothell wasn't expecting to have to feed so many passengers."

Mrs. Bothell invited Miss Yarno to eat, but the O'Conner was tooting the *Squak's* whistle impatiently before the women had finished their meal. Unconcerned, Mrs. Bothell told Miss Yarno, "Never mind, dearie, they won't go until you finish."

The *Squak* finally reached Lake Sammamish's head at 10 p.m.

While the *Squak* made a vital contribution to Eastside settlers' early years, as docks were built, she was eventually replaced by more aesthetically pleasing, less utilitarian craft. Houghton's Curtis family operated the vessel toward the end hauling lumber for Kirkland's Standard Mill. The first boat built and operated on the lake came to her end there, on Christmas Day, 1890, during a windstorm. Tied to the Standard Mill dock, she was battered by waves and sank in shallow water. Her hull was a total wreck, so the frugal owners removed the valuable boiler, which they later used to power mill machinery. Fifteen years later, when Kirkland was incorporated, one of the new town's first orders of business was removing the *Squak's* carcass. The settlers' reliable old friend had become an eyesore.

As engineer of the *Squak*, Houghton resident Wells Green's (b.1861) primary job was to keep the boiler from exploding, which would kill everyone on the little vessel. Green was later the master of the *Urania* (built in 1907).

Houghton was named to honor the Boston family who donated this bell, seen here in 1974, to the area's first church. The Congregational Church of Kirkland still uses the bell which came to the fledgling settlement in 1881.

According to one expert on local history, people have actually had shouting matches over how Houghton got its name.

Some, including the pioneering historian Clarence Bagley in his 1929 *History of King County*, claim Houghton was named for the Houghton brothers, two loggers who lived in the area. The other side backs the bell story, which has it that Houghton was named for a Boston family which bought the struggling young settlement on the frontier a fine bell for their new church. Personally, I believe the bell story.

In 1879, two of Seattle's 3,500 inhabitants were the Reverend and Mrs. Greene. When Greene heard that a small settlement across the lake didn't have a church he and his friend, Mr. Harrison, hiked through the tall trees between Seattle and the water, crossed the lake in a rowboat and landed at the French family's beach. The Frenches were just sitting down to supper, so they invited Greene and Harrison to join them.

The following Sunday, over 40 people, most of the area's residents, greeted Greene when he returned. He preached his sermon at the French cabin, promising to return to the settlement, then called Pleasant Bay, every two weeks thereafter. In this was he established the First Church of Christ of Pleasant Bay.

Initially, the congregation met in Harry French's cabin—which also served as a schoolhouse during the week—but agreed to build a permanent church building. Harry French donated a plot of land for the structure, which was completed using donated materials and volunteer labor. Shortly after residents completed the church, Mrs. Green received a letter from Sarah Houghton, a friend who lived in Boston. Houghton wrote:

"I am very much interested in your church and want you to have a bell. Can't you tell me how much it will cost to get one, not a poor one, but a good one; right in every respect?...If your husband can procure one on the Pacific Coast please let me know at once the cost of the bell, the hanging of the same with its traveling expenses . . . Mr. Houghton can arrange so that the money can be paid in Portland if necessary, or can send a Boston check. Yours Affly, S. J. Houghton."

The Houghtons bought the bell which, with much effort, was carried to the church but sat outside until a belfry was built in 1885. Once hung, it was heard as far away as Juanita. In a 1942 newspaper interview, Vannie Wittenmyer, who lived at Totem Lake (previously called Lake Wittenmyer, or Mud Lake) in the 1880's said, "We could hear the Houghton Bell at our home, and I used to love to listen to it."

The First Church of Christ at Pleasant Bay evolved into today's Congregational Church of Kirkland. They re-hung the Houghton Bell in 1976 and still ring it regularly.

Harry French recounted in his journals that when U.S. Post Office officials told the Pleasant Bay settlers they would have to shorten the community's name to a single word, they chose Houghton, after the family who gave them the fine bell. As Houghton's first permanent settler, who would know better that Harry French how Houghton was named?

Harry French (left) is standing with Rev. Samuel Green in front of his first Houghton home, a simple cabin. The scene is near Lake Washington Boulevard at Marsh Park. The First Church of Christ at Pleasant Bay is behind them. This photo probably dates from the 1880s, since the church was built in 1879. It was demolished in 1974.

The First Church of Christ at Pleasant Bay with belfry and bell in place.

The Hon. John J. McGilvra, Esq. and
Why Madison Park Really Mattered to Kirkland

Seen here in the 1910s, Madison Park had a long history of serving Kirklanders.

Some Kirklanders spent more time passing through Madison Park, the ferry end of the line for them, than they did through parts of their own town. During ferry and steamer days, Kirkland and Seattle's Madison Park neighborhood were close neighbors, so it is worth taking a look back at the other side of the lake.

John J. McGilvra (1827-1903) was Madison Park's first resident. During the 1850s, as a young Chicago-area lawyer, his office adjoined that of another attorney, whose acquaintance led to McGilvra's appointment as Washington Territory's United States Attorney General in 1861. That territory also included part of today's Idaho.

McGilvra was 37-years old when he set up shop in the small mid-Sound lumber camp called Seattle. Despite its small population, he figured that Seattle was on its way up. Seattle had already secured the University of Washington and the Northern Pacific Railroad was considering the town for its terminus. In 1864 McGilvra chose to settle his family on a large land claim on Lake Washington's thickly wooded, uninhabited western shore. Today's address of his house was 1500 42nd Ave N. McGilvra named his spread Laurel Shade and soon used his personal funds, $1500, to cut a trail through the woods connecting it to Seattle. He called the trail the Lake Washington Wagon Road. That trail was later named Madison Street by Seattle co-founder Arthur A. Denny, to honor President James Madison. It was Seattle's only street serving as a direct route between fresh and salt water.

Harry French and other early Eastside settlers made their first explorations of the lake from Laurel Shade, often borrowing McGilvra's small sailboat. They also called the property "McGilvra's Farm," "McGilvra's Landing," and "McGilvra's Place." The name was also altered, in some references, to "McGilvry's Landing."

Eventually, McGilvra platted his land for development, but he donated 24 acres for public use. First known as "Madison Street Park" it eventually became simply "Madison Park."

A small settlement was developing at Madison Park. In the 1880s and by the 1890s its shoreline was a popular steamer landing, houseboat community and a resort area. Connected to Seattle by a streetcar line operated by the Madison Street Cable Railway Company, which John J. McGilvra had formed, Madison Park offered patrons swimming beaches, a dance pavilion and other amusement park diversions. Some were bizarre, like the booth operated by a black man named Smoky Joe, who allowed people to punch him in the face—as hard as they wanted—for one dollar.

The turn-of-the-century brought the King County ferry dock to Madison Park and, after 1910, Kirkland's Realtors Burke and Farrar set up an office there promoting Kirkland real estate.

Madison Park continued to serve as Kirkland's connection Madison Park and Seattle until the last ferry run, in 1950.

A final note about McGilvra: his friend who appointed him United States Attorney for the Territory of Washington in 1861 was a tall fellow, raised out in the Kentucky and Illinois woods. He was named Abraham Lincoln.

John J McGilvra, late of the firm McGilvra, Blain & DeVries. In 1893 McGilvra was described as: "..the oldest member of the legal profession in Seattle, Washington, both in years and practice" and "the father of the Seattle bar." He served in the Territorial Legislature in 1866-67, and procured funds for a wagon road across the Cascades through Snoqulamie Pass.

Laurel Shade was John J. McGilvra's 1864 home at today's Madison Park.

A 1939 view of the Madison Park-Kirkland ferry dock and Madison Park swimming beach.

The lake steamer *Urania* in 1913 at Madison Park. As it became clear that the horseless carriage was here to stay, owner Captain Anderson had her modified to accommodate vehicles.

Madison Park on Lake Washington, Seattle, Wash.

Madison Park in the 1910s.

The Hartig house in North Juanita was built in 1912 as a 'gentleman's farm.' In 1994 it still looked much as it had in the 1900s, both inside and out.

Around 1908, a newly married young couple, Rowan and Ada Walters, moved from North Carolina to the Midlakes area of Bellevue, where they established Walters Grain and Feed store.

Within a few years they had a daughter, Hazel. Occasionally Ada took young Hazel to visit a family named Hartig who lived on a 10-acre farm in north Juanita. The families eventually fell out of touch, but the Hartig house still stands today.

George (1858-1936) and Liberty (1867-1958) Hartig moved to their farm from Seattle, where George owned businesses. Liberty had originally moved to Seattle as a child with her parents in 1877. Suffering from an illness, George's doctor told him to go "out to the country." Juanita was 'country' up until the mid-20th century.

The Hartigs built their house about 1912 and lived there with their four children. Then considered a 'gentleman's farm,' the house was elaborate and well appointed for local standards. In an era when some local residents lived in converted chicken coops, the Hartig property boasted a large, fine home, a barn and several outbuildings, including a blacksmith's shed.

The Hartigs grew grapes and lived on the farm for the rest of their days, passing the property on to their daughter, Georgie Chase, a widow. In 1964, South Juanita resident Colleen Granger and her family began looking for a new old house to buy but found nothing they liked until the Hartig property became available in 1969. By then Chase's health was poor and she had to move from her house. Granger said she decided to purchase the home and a portion of the property sight unseen.

As a convenience to Mrs. Chase, the Grangers told her not to worry about cleaning up the house when she moved. When the Grangers did move in they were in for a big surprise: the house was still furnished its original 1912 appointments: furniture, 1890 Monarch wood and coal stove, stereo photo viewers, a Sanitor wooden icebox, hand-operated water pumps and laundry wringer, three 1912-era telephones, and even an 1895 National Gramophone. The house was an time capsule from the 1910s, a veritable museum.

"Everybody said bulldoze it over," said Granger, since in 1969 older homes were not considered as desirable as they are today. Instead, Granger kept the house original, down to the 1900s calendars which still adorn her walls.

Granger will host the August 31 (1994) Kirkland Heritage Society meeting at 7 p.m. and anyone interested in seeing this fascinating real-life glimpse into Kirkland's past is welcome.

One final note about Granger: her mother was Hazel Walters, the little girl who had made the long trek from Bellevue to play with the Hartig children during the 1910s.

The Hartigs in the 1930s.

229

World War II brought a dramatic increase in activity at the Lake Washington Shipyards. Ship building methods also changed to accelerate production, including a greater reliance on welding over riveting. The yard required nearly 400 gas bottles each day. Marcus and Henry Johnston operated the steamer *Ariel* and hauled full bottles from Seattle and returned with empties.

When strolling through the fine retail businesses and marina at today's Carillon Point, it is hard to believe that this attractive waterfront development was once alive around the clock with industrial activity.

It is important to remember that decades ago, Kirkland, and the Eastside generally, did not have a reputation for being a middle class suburban community, as is the case today. These were solid little towns, with the majority of residents employed in agriculture and trades. Most here lived modestly. The average pre-World War II house contained 950 square feet.

World War II shipyard activity brought a boom to the Kirkland area and with it many changes, both to the town and to the yard itself. Dr. Lorraine McConaghy, in her master's thesis, *The Lake Washington Shipyards: For the Duration*, pointed to how most U.S. shipyards, including Lake Washington, had to alter their production methods to accommodate the US government's massive call for new shipping. Among these changes were standardization of design, fabrication of pre-assembled units, and increased worker specialization.

Prior to the war, shipyards such as Lake Washington had manufactured everything necessary to build the ship on site, "...From the anchor chain to the captain's bed," according to McConaghy. The war brought in sub-contractors for blacksmithing, painting, and other tasks. At the yard, ships were built for the first time in sectional units, assembly-line fashion. Workers repeatedly performed specific tasks, which facilitated quick training of the thousands of new workers flooding into the town. This was in stark contrast to the pre-war system that relied on skilled tradesman who had learned to perform numerous tasks over a period of years.

Technology also changed shipbuilding techniques. The pre-war method of joining two metal plates, riveting, gave way to welding as a simpler and faster method. This change brought about the need for new welders, and many were sent out into the yard as tackers after only a few weeks of training. After gaining more experience, many of these tackers were able to pass the US Navy welding test and go on to more complicated welding tasks.

Both arc (electrical) and gas welding methods were used at the yard, but gas welding required large quantities of oxygen and acetylene, which were, as today, pressurized in steel bottles. To illustrate the amount of work that was going on then, each day during the war the steamer *Ariel* brought 400 gas bottles to the boat yard across the lake from Seattle each day.

The Lake Washington Shipyards had its own newspaper, *On The Ways*, where this photo of the yard at night originally appeared.

A wartime cartoon from *On The Ways*.

Lake Washington Shipyards viewed from the lake, 1944.

The *USS Absecon* (AVP-23) was a United States Navy 1766-ton Barnegat-class seaplane tender constructed at the Lake Washington Shipyards and launched on March 8, 1942. She was unique among the Barnegat-class ships in that she was the only one fitted with an aircraft catapult and cranes for handling floatplanes. She was decommissioned in 1947 and loaned to the US Coast Guard in 1949. She remained in Coast Guard service until 1972 when she was turned over to the Republic of Vietnam. When South Vietnam fell in 1975, she was captured by the North Vietnamese and is believed to have seen use in its navy until 2000.

GARDINERS BAY COMMISSIONED

The *USS Gardiners Bay* (AVP-39) was commissioned February 11, 1945 and was the 23rd seaplane tender built by Lake Washington Shipyards. She earned two battle stars for her World War II service and then four more for service in the Korean Conflict. She was given to Norway in 1958 and was retired in 1974.

Lake Washington Shipyards-built seaplane tender *Timbalier* (YVP-54) seen in action a long, long way from Houghton, with two Martin "Mariner" PBM-3 flying boats.

The *Timbalier* launching at Lake Washington Shipyards, April 18, 1943.

AVP-26
LWS
15-JUNE-43
HOUGHTON, WASH.

1890: The Kirkland News, the incredible Charles "Chuck" Morgan, and Newspapering in Kirkland.

Masthead from the September, 1890 issue of *The Kirkland News*.

The Kirkland News hailed Kirkland as the coming "Pittsburg of the Pacific!"

Since the nation's birth, local newspapers have provided an important community service. As Americans migrated west, establishing a newspaper in a brand new settlement legitimized the fledgling town—it was a sign that the town should be taken seriously.

Today, the *Kirkland Courier* is the only newspaper devoted to Kirkland readers, but it has been preceded by numerous other publications. While reporting news from several Eastside communities, Charles Morgan's *East Side Journal* is undoubtedly the best remembered of Kirkland's newspapers.

Morgan, still an active Kirkland community figure, published the *Journal* for several decades as a well regarded source of local news. Recognizing the importance of Kirkland's past, Morgan often offered readers photographs and stories about local history.

The Kirkland real estate development firm Burke and Farrar created the *Journal* in 1918 and for many years its editor was H. P. Everest, a 1912 Kirkland High School graduate. Other Kirkland papers included the *Kirkland News-Advertiser* (1950s), the *East Side News* (1910s), *The Kirkland Independent* (1910s) and *The Kirkland Press* (1900s).

A lone issue of Kirkland's first newspaper, *The Kirkland News*, still exists in Charles Morgan's private collection. The paper's first issue, dated Sept. 6, 1890, is an incredible glimpse into Kirkland life during its steel mill boom period. It proudly proclaims: "Kirkland is the coming iron metropolis of the world!" Well, you can't believe everything you read in the paper.

Newspaper writing style in 1890 seems awkward by today's standards, as exemplified by a message from the editors, "Its proprietors, both young men, thanking you for the encouragement that you have thus far given them, ask for a continuance of your kindly interest which they will endeavor to reciprocate to the utmost extent of their power."

Most of the front page is a single story about the Snoqualmie Valley, the area from which the Kirk investors planned to mine iron ore. Other stories inside report on the King County Republican convention (Kirkland, Houghton, and Juanita each sent two delegates, Seattle sent 103), Labor Day celebrations, and "facts about butter making."

Local news was a stabbing at Tolt (renamed Carnation in 1917, back to Tolt in 1928 and then, finally, back to Carnation once more in 1951), mill construction at Forbes Lake and brick buildings rising in town, "When these are completed Kirkland will have one more brick residence than Seattle." Advertising included Kirkland lots for $25 where the sellers accurately foretold prospective buyers, "You will never have the opportunity to buy lots so cheap again."

Like Kirk's dream, *The Kirkland News* failed, after publishing only a few issues. Unfortunately, Morgan's is the only know surviving copy. Other issues, if they existed, would undoubtedly provide invaluable information, so anyone coming across one will have made an important find.

"Mr. Kirkland," Charles "Chuck" Morgan (1911-2009).

Intolerable Excuses for Communism

It's amazing how many people are inclined to write off as unimportant the cases of some witnesses who have been requested to appear before Senate and House Un-American Activities Committees. Velde Committee sessions opened in Seattle Monday.

In many instances these witnesses began their affiliations with the Communist influence while attending one of our colleges or universities. In the minds of some, this excuses them.

"Oh, they just get carried away with some of the things they pick up in school," say their "broad-minded" defenders. Not in our book!

It's time we are learning that seeds of Communism are not planted in the minds of stupid freshmen barely able to meet scholastic requirements. Promoters of Communism make the most headway with the bright student and he in turn "sells the deal" to his associates.

Not long ago the University of Washington discovered it had on the faculty some "liberal" professors who sandwiched into their lectures the favorable features of Communism—whatever they might be. These professors were given the heave-ho but the housecleaning wasn't without repercussion. A lot of people thought the professors were being gagged or persecuted. It took some courage on the part of the top administration, including Vice-President Dick Everest, to lower the boom and eliminate these Reds from the teaching roster.

It will be interesting to see how the witnesses in the Velde hearings will crawl and cling to the First and Fifth Amendments.

We are well acquainted with the background of one newspaper man who has been subpoenaed. He was a sharp student at one of our state colleges. He felt hobbled when he couldn't express his opinions in the college paper, so he started one of his own. Its columns were loaded with the old liberal slush. Some of the top administrative brass called his "intellectual" writings "free thinking" and didn't appear too disturbed over the publication of his little paper, "Upstream".

When the story of this student's activities appeared in the college alumni magazine and Upstream's editor was criticized in the alumni journal, it was surprising how many people complained of our attempts to thwart "free intellectual thinking." We know because we wrote the story. That was back in 1939. It was evident then that the Communist patter

had real appeal to him. Now, 15 years later, he is being called to testify before the House Un-American Committee on his long tenure as editor of the People's World.

There's no excuse for the nation's youth to be carried away by some professor's intellectual treatise on Communism, even though his approach is clever and the pill is sugar-coated. Any theory in contradiction to the Pledge of Allegiance should be spotted easily by a college student. The wording is very simple:

"I pledge allegiance to the flag of the United States and to the Republic for which it stands." There's nothing tricky about that. It means you are for the U.S.A. 100 percent.

"One Nation indivisible with Liberty and Justice for all."

Congress is studying the addition of two words to the pledge which will make it even more powerful and effective. "Under God" is being recommended as an insert after "One Nation".

Let's face one of the really true, live issues facing the people of the United States today: Communism is an evil. Every effort should be made to remove it. A confirmed Communist believes in the overthrow of government by force. Imagine how quickly this could be accomplished if Communists within cooperated with a Communistic armed force attacking our nation. In one fell swoop they could knock out power and communications and damage could be irreparable.

You'll find that the person who worries about the evils of Communism—who tolerates no part of it and hates it—is pretty well grounded in Americanism.

Let's not be so ready to think of Communism within our nation as just some crack-pot idea being propounded by crackpots. It's a vicious, despicable ideology that should be eliminated as quickly and as thoroughly as possible.

It seems to us that our schools would perform a great service if they taught every pupil that it is a privilege to be an American and that he or she should be happy to stand before any government agency and be able to say, "I am an American. I always have been an American (or have since I became a citizen) and always will be. I'm proud of it and would die for my country."

In this way you engender a positive approach toward good citizenship; an enthusiasm for being proud of being an American. We want no part of anyone who isn't, all the way, right to the core.

An East Side Journal policy editorial, June 17, 1954.

240

An article from the September, 1890 issue of *The Kirkland News*.

H. P. "Dick" Everest (1893-1967) seen in 1930, during his years running the *East Side Journal*. Though born in Wisconsin, Everest grew up in Kirkland and graduated from Kirkland High School in 1912 and then from the University of Washington, where he later served as a vice president. Over his career Everest amassed an impressive resume of business, academic, and community achievements.

Diphtheria causes a horrid, lingering death. Almost unimaginably so.

It often kills by asphyxiation; it chokes the life from its victim. It is an acute infectious disease caused by the bacteria *Corynebacterium diphtheriae,* which spreads through respiratory droplets produced by a cough or sneeze of an infected person. The bacteria most commonly infect the nose and throat, the neck often swells and the victim struggles to breathe and swallow. The throat infection causes a gray-black or dirty white, tough, fiber-like covering, a disgusting adherent membrane, which often blocks the airways which, lacking intubation or a tracheotomy, kills the victim. Once infected, toxins, produced by the bacteria, can spread through the victim's bloodstream to other organs, such as the heart, and cause death. Once quite common, diphtheria has been eradicated, mostly, in industrialized nations through vaccinations. But this was not the case in 1882….

The Union 'A' High School at Kirkland. The Clark's land patent, awarding them hard-won title to their homestead in today's Highlands neighborhood.

Martin and Eliza Clark, 28 and 26, came to San Francisco from Iowa by the transcontinental railroad in 1876 or possibly 1877, and from San Francisco took a sailing ship to Seattle with their two daughters, Sarah, 2, and Ora, 4.

According to their youngest son, Dr. Charles Walter Clarke, MD, writing years later, Eliza was petite, about five feet tall, with blond hair and a "merry disposition." He described his mother as a devout Christian and a devoted wife and mother who came from pioneer stock. She was a descendant of Mayflower pilgrim Edward Doty, one of two indentured servants obligated to a tanner and merchant named Stephen Hopkins. Doty also signed the Mayflower Compact. Elisa's later ancestors were among the first settlers in Ohio, who later pushed west to the then-frontier of Illinois and later Iowa.

Highlands Neighborhood pioneer Eliza Clark
on her Kirkland homestead, c late 1800s

Martin's ancestors were also early colonial settlers, arriving in Massachusetts in 1635 and later pressing on to Vermont, New York, and finally Iowa in 1854. Also a devout Christian, Martin was, like his father, a cobbler who hand-crafted fine shoes. But the prospect of independence, opportunity, and free land under the Homestead Act lured Martin to bring his young family to the wild frontier that was Washington Territory in the 1870s.

The family staked a claim near Green Lake, then well outside Seattle's city limits. They built a cabin and made other improvements required by the government for a settler to gain title under the Homestead Act. Soon Eliza gave birth to a boy, Willis. But prior to *proving up*, the term for the process of gaining title to the land, the claim's poor soil and other factors prompted Martin to sell his rights, for $175. In October, 1882, the Clarks moved east, across Lake Washington, to the dark primeval coniferous forest that then covered the Eastside.

243

Martin staked out 154 acres in what is today's Highlands Neighborhood. The Clark's claim was the hill and swampy bottom land below it. The claim contained less timber than most Eastside homesteads—Martin estimated there was fewer than 100,000 board feet on the land. And, like most of Kirkland, the soil was third-rate, composed mainly of sandy loam

Walter described his parents' homestead: "Over mile after mile after mile stretched tall fir trees and hardly less imposing cedars. Measuring four to six feet in diameter at the height of a man, the firs towered one to two hundred feet toward the sky. Between these forest giants were smaller trees and shrubs—alders, hazel nut, willows, maples and ash. The forest floor was carpeted with vines and moss. Wild flowers grew in sunny spots. The terrain was a series of hills and valleys. In the valleys ran cool clean water abounding in brook trout and frogs. Large ferns decorated the margins of these streams about the deeper pools rushes and lilies crept from the marshy edges into the limpid water. Birds, rabbits, an occasional harmless snake and too friendly skunks inhabited the forest near the lake, but deep in the wilderness were black and brown bears. Those trappers and prospectors who penetrated the farthest into the forest told of hearing the blood-curdling scream of the cougar."

While Eliza and the children waited in Seattle, Martin readied their "ranch." He cut what he called a road—today we'd call it a trail—three-quarters of a mile long, from the lake to their claim. As the site for their cabin he picked a hill in the center of their land. To make room for the new cabin he had to cut down two massive trees. This he did with the help of a friend and a double bitted ax and a ten-foot crosscut saw, or *misery whip* as these iconic tools were called. The mammoth trunks could not be used as timber, for there was no way to move them. To clear the logs and debris from their home site, Martin simply burned the logs and the stumps where they lay.

Dr. Charles Walter "Walter" Clarke and his sister Margaret (Clark) Habernal c.1910 with Margaret's daughter Theodora (Habernal) Wales. Dr. Clarke crafted a semi-fictionalized account of the Clark tragedy, wherein some names were changed, but homestead and other records confirm the events of those sad days in 1882. According to Clark decedents, Dr Clarke added an 'e' to his last name for professional reasons.

With the clearing completed, Martin brought rough cedar boards and shingles across from a Seattle mill in his rowboat and built a cabin about ten feet high and 24 by 26 feet, with four small rooms and two windows facing west. He also built and populated a chicken house, and for the children he fashioned a cradle and cribs.

Then Martin fetched his family. Walter wrote that Martin hefted Willis to his shoulders, tucked bundles under his arms, seized bags in his hands and led the way up the trail to the cabin while Eliza followed leading Sarah and Ora by their hands and carrying baskets and clothing under her arms. Each little girl dutifully carried some piece of kitchenware as they trudged up the muddy trail.

Walter recorded his mother's reaction to her first glimpse of their homestead: "It's wonderful, Martin. I'm glad we are home."

Neighbors were few and widely scattered. The John DeMott family claim, about a mile away, was the present location of Kirkland's downtown. About a mile east of the Clark's homestead lived a native family. Walter referred to them as "Siwash," a Chinook trade language term for Indians, derived from the French word *sauvage* for 'savage.' Walter described the couple as "…harmless people but ignorant and dirty" and their dwelling as a "hut" constructed of cedar bark. He wrote they were "old" and were called Sam and Mabel. They lived mostly on a diet of the fish they caught. These condescending words are some of the few early observations of native habitation recorded about Native Americans who lived among early Kirkland settlers, and were probably typical of the time.

Bill Perrault, a mysterious and fascinating character, lived about five miles to the east, deeper in the forest. Bill was a tall French-Canadian trapper who lived alone in a remote shack with his many hunting dogs. He made his living selling animal pelts he collected on his trap lines. Though other area settlers viewed Perrault with suspicion, because he had no interest in improving land, the Clarks offered him friendship and hospitality.

Their Eastside forest ranch generated no revenue, so Martin earned his living in Seattle as a shoemaker, staying in a boardinghouse weekdays and returning home on the weekends. Apprehensive about leaving Eliza and the children alone, Martin acquired a sizable dog they named Job and a double barrel black-powder shotgun of unrecorded gauge. Martin taught Eliza to fire the scattergun, but she didn't care for it--being petite the recoil hurt her shoulder. The shotgun was stored loaded on the wall near the stove to keep its powder dry. Job was large and the cabin small and filled with the family, so Job was an outdoor dog. He would often howl at night at the unseen and unheard off in the darkness.

One night when Martin was in town Eliza heard a sound she thought was someone trying the cabin door. Nearly eight months pregnant, deep in the wilderness with her small children, her imagination conjured frightening scenarios involving Indians trying to harm them. Though Puget Sound-area Indians were typically peaceful people, there were occasional alcohol-related incidents of the type also frequently seen in the white population—especially among the young lumberjacks and seamen. Eliza arose from bed, dressed and examined the door and looked out the windows into the darkness, straining to see an intruder. In the twinkling firelight of the woodstove's dying embers, she saw a blurred, shadowy shape and shining eyes. Panicked, she pulled the double barrel shotgun from its hook, raised the butt to her shoulder, pulled the trigger.

Ka-BAAAM! Eliza discharged a barrel and pellets blasted out the window's glass. Black powder smoke and stench filled the cabin. The face vanished. Her shoulder throbbed from the recoil and the children were screaming and crying, awakened by the report. Dropping the shotgun, Eliza embraced her terrified children.

Little Lutie grew up to be a beautiful woman, seen here in 1904. In 1905 she married Ollis Patty, who had stopped in Kirkland to visit family briefly on his way to Alaska. Quite understandably, meeting young Lutie changed his plans--he canceled the trip, married her and the couple had four children. In 1905, Ollis became Kirkland's first City Treasurer, a position he held for about 40 years. Also in 1905, Lutie and Jennie Lowe were Kirkland High School's very first graduates. Lowe was unable to attend commencement, so Lutie received the very first KHS diploma alone on the stage. It is also interesting to note that Lutie is not wearing cosmetics, she was just a naturally very striking woman--then considered 'paint', wearing makeup was not considered socially acceptable by women of 'good' reputation, usually limited at that time to women who worked in the 'theatres' and saloons of Seattle's infamous Tenderloin District.

Martin stayed home after Job's death because Eliza would soon give birth to their fourth child. There was plenty to do. He needed to plant a garden and resume the endless task of clearing his land.

Jeannie DeMott served as midwife for the birth of the new baby, a healthy girl they named Lucy, after Martin's mother. Her siblings called her "Lutie," and that she remained for the rest of her days.

"It's alright my darlings, nothing shall harm you," she whispered, scooping them up, tucking them all into her bed. She recovered the shotgun and sat on the foot of the bed, cradling it in her lap as she spent the remainder of the night with her finger on the gun's second trigger, listening and watching the door and windows attentively.

As dawn illuminated the east, fingers of warm light began poking through the primeval forest. Eliza dreaded walking out the cabin's door into the clearing, convinced she'd see the intruder's bloody corpse splayed on the ground.

Morning's light filled the cabin. Eliza finally forced herself to arise and walk to the now glassless window through which she'd killed the intruder. She peered out and her eyes adjusted to the light. She saw no lifeless Indian, no white prowler, no bear or cougar. To her horror, she had killed their beloved dog, Job.

Eliza late in life, c. 1920

As one of the first babies born to area settlers, Lutie drew gift-bearing visitors from neighboring homesteads. One day buckskin-clad trapper Bill Perrault appeared near the garden with his lever-action rifle resting over his shoulder and a bundle under his arm. After Martin greeted him, Perrault said, "Me I bring a petit cadeau for baby," handing his gift to Eliza--a small, soft squirrel pelt rug which fit perfectly atop baby Lutie in her cradle.

That autumn, after returning home from Sunday services the two older girls complained of sore throats. Eliza, thinking they had colds, rubbed their necks with camphor-impregnated chicken fat and wrapped them in woolen stockings.

But the girls did not improve. Martin felt their feverish heads and peered down their red, inflamed throats. Eliza gave them sweetened water and put them to bed. But the girls tossed in their cribs all night and by morning it was obvious they were seriously ill. Martin looked at their throats again. The inflammation and redness was gone, replaced with an ugly, dirty white membrane that their tonsils and descended their throats. No longer feverish, the girls felt cold.

Martin raced down his trail to the DeMott's place. "Grandma" DeMott was experienced with sickness and remedies. Martin hoped she could help his little girls. After he described their symptoms she looked at him gravely.

247

"Martin, your little girls have malignant croup or diphtheria as they call it now. It is going around Seattle and is very catching. I cannot come help you as I might bring the disease home to my grandchildren, it is terribly dangerous." She sent Martin home with an 'essence' that was to be boiled in water, instructing that the girls must breathe the vapor. As Martin left, Grandma DeMott said, "I will pray for you."

When Martin returned home the girls' breathing was labored and they struggled for breath. Eliza was desperately trying to comfort them. Martin boiled water and essence in a pan and when he lifted little Sarah's head so she could breathe the vapors she managed a weak smile for her dad. When Ora's turn came she was far less responsive. The Clarks continued the vapor treatment throughout the day, but by evening Ora was seized by coughing, vomiting, and breathlessness. After midnight Ora slipped away. Her face turned purple, and, straining to breathe, she died. Martin carried his nine-year-old to the bed of he and Elize and covered her with a clean sheet.

Exhausted and in shock, Eliza watched Martin embraced her and reminded her that they had to focus on saving their other daughter. Through the night and into the next day they desperately administered the steaming essence vapors to Sarah. But as night fell, the six-year-olde slipped away and joined her older sister in death.

Martin and Elizawere paralyzed with grief. Willis called from his bed for a drink. Martin rose and brought his only son a cup of water. To Martin's horror, the boy fingered his neck. His throat hur. Bringing an oil lamp nearer, Martin examined Willis' throat. It was red and inflamed. The Clarks boiled more essence and had the boy breathe the vapors. It was all they knew to do.

A soft knock at the cabin door revealed Bill Perrault, distressed, fur cap in hand, ready to help his friends, unfazed that he was exposing himself to the deadly diphtheria. Perrault asked what could he do and Martin sent him to Seattle, in the desperate hope he might return with a doctor. The trapper sprinted down the trail to the lake, returning hours later with bad news: no one would come to help the Clarks.

As Perrault and Martin struggled to save the boy, Eliza passed out from exhaustion and shock. Though encouraged by the fact that Willis didn't struggle to breathe as his sisters had—the girls died of asphyxiation—his ashen complexion was an ominous sign. Rapidly accumulating toxins were attacking the little boy's organs. Martin held the steaming essence pan and Perrault lifted the boy from the crib and held him over it to breathe the vapors. But Willis had stopped breathing. His eyes were closed. Martin pressed his hand on his limp, motionless son's small ches. There was no heartbeat. The three-year-old was dead.

Martin shouted in grief, awakening Eliza, who sprang from the bed and ran to her son's side. Barely audible, the devastated woman whispered,"Our little boy is dead!"

Tears streaming down her face, Eliza dashed from the cabin into the dawn. Martin followed her a little knoll that today provides a beautiful view of downtown Kirkland, the lake, the Seattle skyline, and Olympic Mountains on the horizon. Martin held his wife.

"If I could only go with them!" she sobbed.

"We still have little Lutie, she needs you, and so do I," Martin replied.

Bill Perrault dug three small graves. With cedar boards left over from building the cabin, Martin made coffins for his children. Eliza dressed them in their Sunday clothes and changed into her best dress. Martin donned his Sunday suit and then placed the bodies of Ora, Sarah, and Willis in their coffins and carried them to the their graves on the sunny knoll. The Clarks and Perrault read verses from the *Holy Bible* and they prayed, and then were silent for a time. Finally, Eliza gathered Lutie and with Martin returned to their cabin. Bill Perrault remained behind and filled in the three small graves. When he finished, he stopped at the cabin, bid the Clarks goodbye and disappeared into the dark forest.

Eliza awoke with a sore throat the next morning. Desperate, Martin decided to take her into Seattle. As he hastily constructed a litter from saplings, Perrault arrived and when Martin asked for his help, and the Frenchman replied, "Mais oui, certainement."

The men carried Eliza and Lutie down the trail to Martin's boat and rowed the five miles across the lake, finally carrying them another four miles down a muddy trail called Madison Street today and into the smelly, smoky little sawmill settlement of Seattle.

Martin's worst fears were realized. Seattle's one hospital refused diphtheria cases and no hotel or other lodging allowed them accommodations. They slogged desperately over Seattle's notorious deep muddy roads with the sick woman and the infant. The epidemic monopolized Seattle's few doctors. Residents, fearing diphtheria with good reason, offered no assistance. With darkness approaching, with no shelter at hand, and in despair, a kind woman approached and asked, "Are you in trouble?"

The woman wore a nun's habit. The sister approached and Martin and Perrault described their plight.

Lutie, Margaret and Walter, on Eliza's knee, seen c. 1887 on the family homestead. The background suggests the family was still clearing their land.

249

"Come with me, we will care for your wife and child."

Years later Walter wrote that Martin described their rescue by the nun as a miracle. The nuns found a doctor who would treat the woman and her baby. Eliza recovered, and Lutie never showed symptoms of the disease that killed her siblings.

After Eliza recovered Martin rented a house in Seattle for the three of them and he returned to shoemaking. An affidavit in their homestead file states that they remained in town for about four months. Martin and Eliza now faced an important decision. Would they return to their homestead and its haunting reminder of their pain or would they start fresh elsewhere?

Well earned happiness. Martin Clark with his granddaughter Margaret Alice (Patty) Fessenden (1906-96). After their tragedy, the Clarks took great joy in their children and grandchildren.

Martin put this question to Eliza and she did not hesitate. They would to return to their ranch. She intended to plant flowers near the graves. She would not leave her children.

With Bill Perrault's help, the family did return and began anew. The Clarks had two more children: Margaret, born in 1885, and Charles Walter—who Martin nicknamed "Captain" —born in 1888. They also took in and raised two abandoned kids, John Royle and Mary Clark (not related).

As time went on Kirkland grew. Like most of Kirkland's homesteaders, the Clarks sold portions of their 154 acre claim to pay taxes and other obligations incurred during the tough depression years following the 1892-3 failure of Peter Kirk's steel mill. The Clarks were among the founding members of the First Baptist Church of Kirkland, which began in Houghton in 1888 and moved to Fifth Avenue, across from today's Kirkland City Hall, in 1889. The Kirkland Cemetery was established in 1888 and at some point after that the three Clark children who died in 1882 were removed from their graves and moved there where they rest today with their parents, older sister Lutie, her husband Ollis Patty, and their daughter Stella Patty.

A sad, final footnote to the Clark story is the census record that reveals that another of the Clark children died in childhood, likely in Iowa, before the family came west. Many of Kirkland's settlers lived with similar heartbreak. Such losses, unimaginable today, were part of life for Washington Territory's pioneers.

Most of the Clark family rest together today in the Kirkland Cemetery. Margaret Habernal is with them there as well. Eliza was true to her word, she and Martin never left the children they lost in 1882.

Note: This article was informed by an account written by the late Dr. Charles Walter Clarke, MD. For reasons unknown, he changed his surname's spelling to 'Clarke.' All dialogue and related details came from his account. Federal census data also contributed, as did the Clark's Government Land Office (GLO) land file, opened in 1883 and completed in 1888. It was recently purchased by the Kirkland Heritage Society (KHS) and contains an abundance of fascinating detail about the Clark family's early years in Kirkland. KHS recently ordered GLO files for a large number of Kirkland pioneers, primarily of those who settled the three newly annexed neighborhoods. Heartfelt thanks to Patty (Fessenden) Bernhardt, Lutie (Clark) Patty's granddaughter, for her generous donation to KHS of precious family photos, including several of her grandparents and great grandparents, Martin and Eliza Clark. Special thanks to my amazing friend Marianne Reinsfelder for her inspiring support and encouragement with this article. (Originally appeared on Kirklandviews.com, June, 11, 2011).

251

Lutie's granddaughter, Patty (Fessenden) Barnhardt with Matt McCauley in 2010 at the Kirkland Heritage Society Resource Center. Mrs. Barnhardt has kindly donated many items that have helped bring to life the story of her Kirkland pioneer family. (*Loita Hawkinson photo*)

One of the first babies born in today's Kirkland, little Walter Clark grew up, becoming Dr C. Walter Clarke, and in spite of the tragedy his family experienced, Walter grew up to become a distinguished, award-winning physician, medical researcher, and president of the American Social Health Association, dedicating his career to the eradication of the enormous human suffering caused by venereal disease.

Narrators

I interviewed many area seniors when I wrote these columns. All were great, but several stood out, because of the time they graciously gave me and the richness of the photos and material they loaned for duplication. The people below were very special and I wanted to underscore their contributions to this project. They brought many of these stories to life for me.

JoAnn (Johnson) McAuliffe (1937-2007) was an exceptional woman whom I knew all my life. She was a direct descendent of Julius and Anna Ostberg, the couple who purchased Rowland Langdon's 1877 Juanita homestead in the 1900s. She grew up on that property where she and her husband, Jerry McAuliffe, founded McAuliffe's Nursery in 1957. The two retired to Seabeck in 2001 and sold the land to the City of Kirkland for McAuliffe Park.

Mrs. McAuliffe was a wife, a mom and a grandmother—I went to school with her kids and the McAuliffe and McCauley families enjoyed a close association over the past 50 years. She graduated from Lake Washington High School in 1954 and earned her BA from Seattle University in 1957. She was an avid golfer and enjoyed travel.

I interviewed her a number of times and she was full of wonderful, colorful details from a lifetime in Juanita and shared a number of images that are reproduced in this book. We lost Mrs. McAuliffe far too early, but I am at least gratified that before she passed we were able to record many of her memories and perspective on Juanita's past.

JoAnn (Johnson) McAuliffe, center, at Juanita Beach, June, 1953, with friends Marilyn (Timmerman) Johnson, left, and Joanne (Forbes) Deligan, right.

A very precocious little JoAnn (Johnson) McAuliffe seen in the very early 1940s with Mr. and Mrs. Carlson, who lived in the red brick house that still stands on N.E. 116th Street, now a part of McAuliffe Park.

Seen here about 1940 with her maternal pioneer grandmother, Anna Ostberg—an enormously popular woman among Juanita schoolchildren in the first decades of the 20th century.

Dorris (Forbes) Beecher (1913-2006) was the granddaughter of Dorr and Eliza Forbes, the first family to settle on Juanita Bay. She grew up in Juanita and her parents, Les and Alicia, founded Juanita Beach and various other area enterprises. She was a true pleasure to interview, had a sharp mind, a quick wit, and a genuine interest in the events of Kirkland's past. Her grandfather died when she was small, but her memories of her grandmother were clear and vivid—and very entertaining. Through Mrs. Beecher I got a great sense of what this wonderful pioneer woman must have been like.

Dorris (Forbes) Beecher as a senior at Union 'A' High School in Kirkland. She also served as the President of the Class of '32.

And during a 1999 Juanita visit.

255

Don Barrie (1909-1993) and Mabel (Turtainen) Barrie (1912-2005) were great to visit with because Mr. Barrie knew me as a student at A. G. Bell Elementary, going all the way back to kindergarten, in 1969. Mr. Barrie's father and grandfather came to Kirkland in the 1890s to work in the Eyanson woolen mill. Several members of his family were very well known around Kirkland. Mrs. Barrie also grew up in the area and attended the old Juanita Elementary School. Her ancestry was Finnish and she provided some great perspective on that once-thriving community. Mr. Barrie attended the old Central School and then graduated from Kirkland High School in 1928. Mrs. Barrie was in the Class of 1931.

Mr. Barrie worked at the Lake Washington Shipyards after high school and during World War II and as a kid I was fascinated by those stories. While he was performing his custodial duties at the school I often followed him around and pestered him with questions, which he always answered, no matter how busy he was.

Don Barrie, in 1913, sawing firewood. He grew up in Kirkland's West of Market Neighborhood at 410 13th Ave. W.

High school senior portrait, 1928.

Mabel (Turtainen) Barrie as an infant and as a high school senior in 1931.

Don and Mabel Barrie in 1970. Both were avid hikers who loved being in the mountains.

Author Matthew McCauley with O.L. "Deep" Higginbotham, in 1993.

My friend Deep died a few months after my December 8, 1993 column, in which I wrote about him. I wrote an obituary, which appeared in *The Kirkland Courier*, March 9, 1994.

Orval L. 'Deep' Higginbotham (1903-1994).

Former Kirklander Orval "Deep" Higginbotham, 90, died on Feb. 27. He was buried at Floral Hills Cemetery, in Lynnwood, on March 5. Mr. Higginbotham was born in Hillsboro, Ore., on April 6, 1903. His family soon moved to Seattle and then to Juanita in 1919.

In Juanita, Mr. Higginbotham began a semi-pro baseball career that spanned 28 years. He played for the Juanita and Kirkland town teams, as well as numerous other Eastside ball clubs. With a lifetime batting average was over .300, he usually played shortstop and batted leadoff.

In addition to his baseball career, Mr. Higginbotham worked for many years at the Matzen Woolen Mill and other Kirkland businesses. He had a great fondness for sharing stories of his past and volunteered as a narrator for the Kirkland History Project during the last year of his life. Several of those interviews were recorded on tape and archived at the Marymoor Museum.

Mr. Higginbotham also had a large collection of local historic materials, many of which he generously donated to the project for duplication.

He is survived by his wife of 65 years, Kirkland native Florence (Peterson) Higginbotham; son Donald and his wife, Joan, of Steilacoom; daughters, Carol and her husband Al Barker, of Trail, British Columbia; Marjorie Gates, of Bothell; Brother, Irving, of Bothell; sisters, Doris Steinhoff, of Seattle, and Mary Tyler, of Bothell. He has seven grandchildren and 12 great-grandchildren.

He was the owner of Pontius Nursery in Bothell. After he retired he enjoyed fishing and listening to 1920's vintage music on the record player he originally brought across on the ferry for his mother in 1919. Deep Higginbotham helped earn Kirkland its long-standing reputation as a baseball town. He will be dearly missed.

Deep Higginbotham. In 1993 he told the author that during prohibition he knew each of Juanita's bootleggers and where they hid their hooch. He explained the difference between what a moonshiner did as distinguished from the bootlegger—basically, the moonshiner was in manufacturing and the bootlegger was in sales.

About the Author

Matt McCauley's family built a house on Juanita's Little Finn Hill in 1963, the year before his birth. His parents, great aunt and uncle, grandparents, and aunt and uncle purchased several acres of land from Charles and Helma Fowler, who had resided there since the early 1930s. After clearing the land themselves, with chain saws and bulldozers, family members built, one after another, four homes, in which they lived for years.

Their land was part of Juanita's first land plat, which was filed in February, 1912 by Charles B. Harris as Harris Juanita Acres. When Matt was a young boy, Juanita was part of unincorporated King County and it still had a rural sensibility. In his early years he was surrounded by woods, undeveloped wetlands, livestock grazing in pastures, dirt roads with wheel ruts, and a scattering of neighbors, most of whom knew one another. He attended A.G. Bell Elementary from 1969 until 1976, where he played soccer and baseball. As a child he was fascinated with the stories of old Kirkland that he heard from community elders, which inspired his searches in old barns and pastures for treasures of that other time.

Matt moved to Mercer Island in 1976 and graduated from Mercer Island High School in 1982. He learned to SCUBA dive in 1978, and that enabled a lifelong fascination with exploration of Lake Washington and Puget Sound, most especially vessel and aircraft wrecks, and other points of historic interest. He received considerable media attention in 1984-85 when he and high school friend, Jeff Hummel, were sued by the US Navy for salvaging a World War II naval dive bomber from the lake. The two won the suit and went on to recover four other World War II military aircraft in 1987. He returned to Kirkland in 1988 and participated in the Kirkland Heritage Society's 1993 resurrection. He was the founding editor of its award-winning newsletter, *Blackberry Preserves*. That year he began publishing his popular "A Look to the Past" history columns in *The Kirkland Courier*.

McCauley is an alumnus of both Seattle University, where he majored in journalism, and Seattle University School of Law. He lived on the east coast for 13 years, where he owned a business comprising 20 espresso cafes and a commercial coffee roasting plant. He returned to Kirkland in 2010 and lives in Juanita with his sons, Cam, 12, and Jake, 14. Many members of his extended family remain in the Juanita and Finn Hill communities. His father, writer William McCauley, edited this book. He resides in Auburn.

Index

263

40194919R00155

Made in the USA
Charleston, SC
26 March 2015